BEST SEAT IN THE HOUSE

BEST SEAT IN THE HOUSE

18 GOLDEN LESSONS FROM A FATHER TO HIS SON

JACK NICKLAUS II
AND DON YAEGER

W Publishing Group
An Imprint of Thomas Nelson

Published in Nashville, Tennessee, by W Publishing Group, an imprint of Thomas Nelson.

Thomas Nelson titles may be purchased in bulk for educational, business, fund-raising, or sales promotional use. For information, please email SpecialMarkets@ThomasNelson.com.

All photos are provided courtesy of Nicklaus Family Archives.

ISBN 978-0-7852-4837-8 (TP)

Library of Congress Control Number: 2021932184

ISBN 978-0-7852-4836-1 (HC)
ISBN 978-0-7852-4838-5 (eBook)

Printed in the United States of America

22 23 24 25 26 LSC 10 9 8 7 6 5 4 3 2 1

For my wife, Alli, with love

CONTENTS

FOREWORD

I can think of no nicer compliment than to be asked by your son to write the foreword to a book that he has written. When Jackie asked me to consider this—to honor my legacy—I was blown away. It brought back special memories of Jackie's birth, his growing-up years, adulthood, and marriage, and now, with children of his own—how fast time flies!

Barbara and I were just twenty-one when Jackie (our first child) was born—and he did not come with an instruction book! We both grew up with loving and caring parents who taught us right from wrong. So we relied mainly on what we learned and retained from the lessons our parents shared with us.

We tried to be the best possible parents, but I think we learned more from Jackie than we ever taught him. We wanted everything to be perfect, but—as in most child-rearing situations—there were always challenges. Along the way we learned ways to inspire, discipline, share experiences, and value something as simple as time together.

When Jackie shared the manuscript with me, I enjoyed reading his words and, frankly, did not realize what the impact of some of our experiences together had meant to him. I will treasure these words forever! How blessed Barbara and I were, and are, to have raised and been a part of the life of such a special son. He may think he has had the *best seat in the house*, but my seat has been very special too.

I hope you enjoy reading *Best Seat in the House* as Jackie shares his insight into what I feel is a treasured father-son relationship.

—*Jack Nicklaus*
January 2021

INTRODUCTION

Learning from the Golden Bear

I arrived in this world on September 23, 1961, in Columbus, Ohio, as the 7-pound, 8.5-ounce firstborn and bundle of joy of married twenty-one-year-olds Jack and Barbara Nicklaus.

Dad wasn't a household name yet by any means, even if he enjoyed a successful career in amateur and college golf at The Ohio State University. Dad won two U.S. Amateur titles in 1959 and 1961 and gained a modicum of national attention in 1960 when he finished second in the U.S. Open behind Arnold Palmer, by two strokes. He came close to winning, but Arnold rallied from a seven-stroke deficit on the final day to overtake Dad.

As a young father holding my little self, Dad had no idea what the future held, nor, frankly, could he have predicted what would come over the next few decades. However, he realized the best competition was in the professional ranks, and so he turned pro just two months after my birth. Since professional golf was not the lucrative career it is today, Dad juggled other jobs. He successfully sold insurance for Ohio State Life and Parker and Company, a brokerage firm out of New York. He also did promotional work for Hercules Slack Company, a pants manufacturer based out of his hometown, Columbus, Ohio.

Dad's first professional tournament was far from a financial windfall. He finished tied for fiftieth—last place—in the Los Angeles Open on January 8, 1962, twenty-one strokes behind the winner. Dad had to split $100 with two other players who tied for that spot in infamy, pocketing just $33.33. (That extra penny went to one of the other guys!) Even as an infant, I traveled with Mom and Dad to tournaments. The car had clothes and golf clubs in the trunk and a Port-A-Crib and diaper pail in the back seat. Boy, I can't imagine the smell! Night visits to a laundromat were as routine for them as practice rounds in preparation for the next tournament were for him.

Nine months after I was born, Dad, a rookie on the PGA Tour, beat Arnold Palmer in a playoff to win the 1962 U.S. Open for his first professional win, which began to fuel the legendary rivalry with "The King." After that loss to Dad, Arnold said of him, "Now that the big guy's out of the cage, everybody better run for cover."[1] The win also ignited Dad's amazing run in major championships that will likely never be matched. The name Jack Nicklaus had become a big deal.

Being named after my father was more of a warm, wonderful tribute than anything else, but following in his footsteps wasn't always easy. Dad recently admitted that if he'd had a crystal ball to allow him to see into the future, he wouldn't have anointed me his namesake. Dad thought it was unfair to knowingly place that pressure on his son. He said his choice for my name had not entered his mind until maybe five or six years after I was born. At that point, Dad had won two Masters (1963 and 1965), claimed the PGA Championship in 1963, and raised his first claret jug at the Open Championship in 1966 to complete the career Grand Slam at the age of twenty-six.

But as big as the Nicklaus name would become on the golf course, he always put his greatest effort into being just Dad. I've been asked many times throughout my life, "What is it like to be Jack Nicklaus's son?" My quick response has always been, "He's just my dad." When I was six years old, somebody asked me what he did for a living. I shrugged and answered, "Nothing. He just plays golf."

While in college at the University of North Carolina at Chapel Hill, I often simply introduced myself as "Jack." I intentionally didn't mention my last name because—even though they'd eventually figure it out—I wanted people to get to know me for who I was instead of treating me as "Jack's son." Thankfully, and more importantly, as Dad's namesake and firstborn, I have learned so much about Dad and myself over time. And by watching the way he's lived his life, I've spent years in the greatest leadership-parenting-marriage classroom one could imagine.

The greatest golfer of his generation, if not all time, known to his fans globally as the Golden Bear, has always made family his number-one priority. Dad says his life's work—117 championships, including a record eighteen major championships; a successful golf-course design business; an unwavering commitment to his wife (and my mom), Barbara; and raising funds for pediatric care for children—was to make his family proud.

"I hope I have delivered on that," Dad said one day when the subject of priorities came up.

And speaking for the rest of my family, let me respond: Dad, we are proud beyond words.

Dad and Mom both turned eighty-one in early 2021, as we

were finishing this book—Dad on January 21, and Mom, the First Lady of Golf, on February 28. They celebrate their sixty-first wedding anniversary on July 23, 2021. I am the oldest of five children, followed by Steve, Nan, Gary, and Michael. My parents' lives revolve around us and their twenty-two grandchildren. In nearly everything Dad does now, he always considers how it will affect his family when he's gone. And both he and Mom strive to exhibit an enduring love, grace, and humility no matter where they go and what they do.

In the spring of 2020, for instance, Dad and Mom tested positive for COVID-19 at the onset of the coronavirus pandemic. It could have been a bad experience at their high-risk age, but, thankfully, they recovered quickly. Mom didn't exhibit any symptoms; Dad had a sore throat and slight cough. They quarantined in their home in North Palm Beach, Florida, for five weeks so as not to put their family and friends at risk.

Dad tested positive on March 13, 2020, the same day the PGA Tour postponed the season due to the spread of the coronavirus. During his time in quarantine, Dad, always concerned and determined to help others, established a charitable campaign aimed at providing personal protective equipment for frontline health care workers.

Through all of Dad's amazing achievements that made him one of the world's most recognized athletes, he made being a parent one of the most important parts of his life. I know we're all accustomed to hearing people say those kinds of words (usually at retirement parties, lifetime achievement ceremonies, or funerals), but I had the best seat in the house to watch this man live out extraordinary lessons.

While I share these lessons with you, I promise you right

now that my parents never once stopped me and said, "Hey, Jackie, file what I'm telling you right now under 'lessons.'" Dad shaped everything about me, and for the first time in his life (and mine!), it's time to share those lessons he passed down to me as his oldest child.

I want to share stories about Dad in these pages and explain how these stories led to lessons about fatherhood. Along with each story and the lesson learned from it, I'll also include some discussion about how I, as a father, carried that lesson forward to my children. These are the takeaways I used to raise my children—and the way I hope they will raise their children. I hope you find value and fun in all of it.

I have so many experiences and memories of our incredible journey—at home, on the golf course, and in business as vice chairman of the Nicklaus Companies, Dad's course design company based in Palm Beach Gardens, Florida. I have watched the decisions Dad has made throughout his life, and I have been impacted greatly by his pledges to and passion for his family, career, gifting, and mentoring. He has always rightly credited Mom with holding down the fort with the family, but in this tribute, I'll share private family stories that show how Dad set a bar for fatherhood that we all can learn from—wisdom that continues to teach and guide me every day.

The influence of fathers on their children should never be underestimated. Dad's father, Charlie, taught him the lessons he continues to live out. To this day, Dad still wants to make his late father proud with the decisions he makes daily. Charlie, who died from pancreatic cancer at the young age of fifty-six, was a pharmacist who owned several pharmacies in Columbus. A stellar athlete himself, Charlie introduced Dad to athletics and golf. Far more important, Grandpa also taught Dad how to live life the right way, how to be a good sport, and that your word is your bond. Dad studied pre-pharmacy at Ohio State before he decided to pursue a professional golf career.

Dad built on those lessons and passed the mantle to me. Even as I turn sixty years old in 2021, I still live for Dad's approval. That's how much I respect him. I think every son, no matter his age, wants to catch his dad's eye and make him proud, or live a life that honors his memory if he's passed on. I wish knowing I have my dad's approval could be enough, but I need to hear it all the time. I want my life—and the Nicklaus name that stretched across my back when I caddied for him—to mean something. I value that reinforcement from Dad. And I believe my five kids value that reinforcement from me.

Because of his career and life, Dad is the first sportsman, and only the fourth person in history, to be awarded the three most significant honors an American civilian can receive: the Presidential Medal of Freedom (2005), the Congressional Gold Medal (2015), and the Lincoln Medal (2018). He is the first living person outside of the royal family to appear on a British banknote. Dad was voted *Golf Magazine's* 2014 Architect of the Year, received the 2017 World Golf Award for Golf Course Designer of the Year, and his company, Nicklaus Design, is responsible for nearly 450 courses open for play worldwide. The Jack Nicklaus Museum is housed on the campus of his alma mater, The Ohio State University, in his hometown of Columbus. There are multiple awards named after Dad as well.

The Jack Nicklaus National Player of the Year Award is presented annually to the top male players in the country from five different collegiate divisions. The Jack Nicklaus Award is presented to the first-year PGA Tour player with the best scoring average, and the Jack Nicklaus Medal is presented to the U.S. Open winner.

Those are just a few of the ways Dad's accomplishments have been recognized, but they all pale in comparison to Mom and Dad's commitment to making a difference in the world. In 2004, they cofounded the Nicklaus Children's Health Care Foundation, which has raised more than $100 million in less than fifteen years, and its impact has led to the rebranding of renowned Miami Children's Hospital and Miami Children's Health System to Nicklaus Children's Hospital. The hospital has cared for families and children from 119 countries and all fifty states. The Nicklaus Children's Health System includes seventeen outpatient and urgent care centers, with plans to grow. Dad credits Mom for her vision and work in this area—Mom was the recipient of the 2019 PGA Distinguished Service Award and the 2015 Bob Jones Award, the U.S. Golf Association's highest honor, which is bestowed on those who show "spirit, personal character, and respect for the game."[2] And this journey has become more personal for Dad over the years as he has grown close to some of the families and children that he and Mom have helped, and these people tug on his heartstrings.

Dad has repeatedly said golf is just a game. Though it turned out to be an important component in his life, he says the miracles he has witnessed in hospitals are far more important than any four-foot putt he ever made.

In 1972, at the age of thirty-two, Dad won the U.S. Open at Pebble Beach Golf Links in Pebble Beach, California. I was ten years old, barely tall enough to see over the gallery rope lines. I sat on the ground near the 17th green, out of the way and behind the cheering spectators, shifting and looking between people's knees and legs to watch my dad (*Golf Digest* captured and published a picture of me in that moment). At the par-3 17th, he hit what would be described as one of the most famous shots in his career. Pulling a 1-iron out of his bag, Dad used it to make a tee shot that hit the green, bounced once, and struck the flagstick. The ball landed inches away from the hole, and Dad tapped in for a birdie. Dad bogeyed the 18th, but it didn't matter. He beat Bruce Crampton by two strokes for his second consecutive major that year.

Though my vantage point was obstructed by all those legs, I had the *best seat in the house* that day for Dad's eleventh career major championship. A few minutes after that victory, I was sitting on Dad's lap when he received a congratulatory telephone call from President Richard Nixon. How many ten-year-olds get to listen in as their fathers talk to the president of the United States?

Although now I'm much taller and older, my view of my dad hasn't changed.

So back to the question, "What is it like to be Jack Nicklaus's son?" I had never pulled back the curtain and given an in-depth answer until I spoke at the Congressional Gold Medal presentation for my dad in 2015. During my speech, I discussed in detail the 1986 Masters, where I served as Dad's caddie. Not many had given Dad a chance at victory because they thought he was past his prime at the age of forty-six, but he proved everyone wrong. He shot a final round of 65, seven shots under par, with a 30 on the back nine, for a total score of 279 to win his record sixth Masters. He became the oldest winner of the Masters and second-oldest winner of any major championship, behind Julius Boros, who at forty-eight won the 1968 PGA Championship.

But that's not the memory etched into my heart. I described it this way after Dad's final putt dropped on the 18th green. (I share more of my speech later in this book.)

> And there I was, completing the mundane task of placing the flag back into the cup. For me, time was standing still as the cheers continued. I was thinking, *Wow, Dad really played great today.* Yet it was more, so much more. This man, this wonderful man, had accomplished so much. He is Jack Nicklaus; he is arguably the greatest golfer in the history of golf. The Golden Bear had just won his sixth green jacket in incredible fashion. His fans adored him. It was his moment in time. A moment so earned and a moment so deserved. . . .
>
> So there I was, turning from the flag, and all I saw was my dad. In the midst of this moment—that was all about Jack Nicklaus—there Dad stood, waiting for me with the most wonderful smile. His arms were outstretched to embrace me. Dad had made me a part of it. I knew I had Dad's full focus. I felt like I mattered. And I felt loved. That is what it's like to be his son.[3]

Whether you are a serious golf fan, a casual golfer, or someone who has never picked up a club before in your life, you will be able to learn lessons from my father. You might recognize some of these lessons from things you've discovered in your own life. Other lessons might be new to you, even if you apply them far away from the golf course.

Now, let's get ready to tee off for eighteen golden lessons.

CHAPTER 1

Listen to Your Children

As parents, we are often living lives filled with distractions, emotional challenges, and professional and personal disruptions. No matter what you face, take every opportunity you are given to listen to your children. My dad did that so well—even when his career was at its peak and he was traveling so much—and his actions toward me taught me to listen to my own children.

On Father's Day in 1980, Jack Nicklaus was doing what he loved most—being a dad.

And I—eighteen years old at the time—was being selfish. I had just completed my second round in a Palm Beach County Junior Golf Association tournament at the Osprey Point Golf Course, located in Boca Raton, Florida, a few miles from our home in North Palm Beach. I was at the scorers' table that late

Sunday afternoon signing my scorecard when somebody yelled over to me that my dad was on the telephone.

I was a little frustrated about the timing of the call because the tourney was still being played. At that moment for me, this junior golf tournament was the most important thing going on in the world. I had just graduated from high school and signed a golf scholarship to play at the University of North Carolina.

I picked up the telephone receiver. Dad asked me how I played.

Well, I hadn't scored very well, but I proceeded to describe my entire round, hole by hole, shot by shot, whether I lifted my head during a swing, misread a putt—whether it went left instead of straight—or if the ball slowed against the grain.

Literally, I went on and on for twenty straight minutes.

Dad listened, patiently and intently. He responded with questions about why I thought I might have made certain mistakes as I rehashed my eighteen holes. When I told him I was having problems with my chipping, he promised we'd work on it when we both got home. He was so interested, generous, and genuinely wanted to hear about it. All of it. As I finally finished, there was a short silence. I was about to thank Dad for calling me and say goodbye.

Then Dad said, "Jackie, would you like to know how your dad did today?"

A little embarrassed, I quickly said, "Well, yes, how did you do today?"

"Well, I just won the U.S. Open."

That was Dad.

The Golden Bear had just set a new tournament scoring record to win his fourth U.S. Open title at Baltusrol Golf Club in Springfield, New Jersey. And he was on the telephone, some twelve hundred miles away, asking *me* how my round went at a junior golf tournament.

I didn't realize it at the time, but Dad taught me a valuable lesson that Father's Day. It's a lesson that I have grown to understand and tried to incorporate into my daily life as a husband and father to five children.

That junior golf tournament has no meaning for me to this day. But Dad's telephone call still resonates deeply.

A good parent always makes time to listen to his or her children.

It's not as easy as it sounds.

Dad could have quickly changed the direction of our conversation that Sunday afternoon forty years ago. That was a big, big day for him, having not won a tournament in 1979, the first year in seventeen he had gone winless as a professional. The experts and pundits believed, at age forty, he was past his prime. But minutes after making history, with a new scoring record, he telephoned me to see how I had played.

That is just one of many examples throughout my life when Dad made me his top priority. He always made a point to arrange his schedule to meet mine. Just as important, Dad was always there to listen. It was only four years later—a few weeks after I graduated from the University of North Carolina—when again I failed to think about Dad and what he might have had going on in his busy life.

I entered the 1985 North and South Men's Amateur Championship. It's an annual invitational tourney that has been held since 1901 at the Pinehurst Resort in North Carolina. It's also a tournament that Dad won in 1959, at age nineteen, while attending Ohio State.

I wasn't a star player by any means during my golf career at North Carolina. Five to eight players compete in college tournaments, and I was usually positioned anywhere from seventh to third in the rotation. I won two college tournaments and wasn't a high-confidence player on the course. Some of my teammates included all-Americans like John Inman, Davis Love, Kurt Beck, Brian Sullivan, and Greg Parker. It was a very competitive team, and I always did my best just to squeeze into the lineup.

I played well that spring and felt good about the North and South tournament. Prior to the event, I traveled to Puerto Rico and stayed ten days with Chi-Chi Rodríguez, who won eight PGA Tour events during his career and, in 1992, was the first Puerto Rican to be inducted into the World Golf Hall of Fame. My short game has always been the weakest component of my game, and Chi-Chi took me under his wing and shared lessons on chipping that hit home with me and helped me improve.

At Pinehurst, the tourney's format is pretty straightforward. The 120-player field competes over two days on both the Pinehurst No. 2 and Pinehurst No. 4 courses. The field is then cut to a 32-player match play bracket, and I played well enough to advance. All match play rounds are contested on Pinehurst No. 2, which stands as one of my favorite courses to this day.

On his way from Florida to Ohio for the upcoming Memorial Tournament, Dad decided to make a pit stop in North Carolina to watch me play. I assumed Dad figured he'd watch me get beat, and then we'd drive together to Dublin, Ohio, for the Memorial Tournament. It was an event Dad founded in 1976, and one he hosts every year on a course he designed at Muirfield Village Golf Club. Dad was also the defending champion that year, and I caddied for him during his 1984 win there.

Well, after Dad arrived in Pinehurst, my good luck continued. I won my next two matches. I overheard Dad's conversation with Mom that evening when he said, "Hey, Barbara, your son won again today. So we're staying over for another night."

I continued to win. Each day after the match, Dad and I hit balls at the range, where he helped me with my swing and fundamentals. After dinner we talked as we walked one or two miles around the grounds at Pinehurst, which was so peaceful, but we didn't say as much about golf as we did about staying focused on a routine. We said our good nights and headed to our quaint bed-and-breakfast–style rooms.

At this point, there were only four players left in the tournament. I was scheduled to play Peter Persons in the semifinals. On paper, I was the underdog. Peter was a premier player at the University of Georgia. He won medalist honors at the Southeastern Conference (SEC) Championship that spring as a senior, was a former Georgia Amateur and Georgia Junior Championship winner, and would later turn professional.

The evening before our match, Dad, Peter, and I enjoyed dinner at the Pine Crest Inn, where we were staying. We had a nice time. However, during our conversation Peter, unprovoked and as if I were not even present, looked at my dad and casually said, "I called my mom tonight. And I let her know that I only brought enough clothes for tomorrow [the semifinals]. I told her she needed to bring me another set of clothes for the finals."

Obviously, if Peter believed he needed another set of clothes for the finals, he was expecting to beat me. I'm sure it was a bit of a mind game, but it was also a funny moment because neither Dad nor I knew how to respond. Dad, not to belittle Peter at all, looked at me innocently and just smiled. No words, just a smile.

During that awkward moment of silence after Peter's subtle prediction, the waitress asked all three of us if we wanted Peach Melba (peaches simmered in a sugar syrup mixture) for dessert. Her question broke the silence, and we all laughed, even Peter.

The next day Peter got off to a nice start in our match, draining a fifteen-foot birdie putt on the 1st hole. As I walked to the 2nd tee, one stroke down, I looked at Peter and told him, "Nice start. That was really a nice birdie." I also caught Dad's eye at the same time; he heard me congratulate Peter. Dad smiled and gave me a thumbs-up as if to say that was the right thing to do as a competitor.

The match went back and forth, but I finished strong and beat Peter four-and-three to advance into the thirty-six-hole finals the following day against Tom McKnight. (I was sure glad I brought an extra set of clothes.) I played well against Tom, birdied two of the last three holes, and beat him to win the tournament, matching Dad's accomplishment twenty-six years earlier. We had a great celebration that night with Dad and Mickey Neal, who was my golf, football, and basketball coach in high school.

I know Dad never expected to be in Pinehurst for as long as he was. While Dad and I never talked about Peter's prediction and his telephone call to his mother to bring additional clothes, I *know* Dad didn't bring enough clothes for his stay. However, not once did he mention the preparation and great responsibilities he had for the next week's Memorial Tournament.

Dad was proud of me and made me believe the North and South Men's Amateur Championship was the most important event in my life—and his. He encouraged me, supported me, and always listened. What's so cool about that victory is that the winner receives Pinehurst's iconic bronze Putter Boy trophy.

What was also great was that Dad and I were featured on the cover of *Golf World* magazine after my victory, with the caption "A trophy of his own."

That is a moment in time I will always treasure.

Of course, there are other moments when Dad was equally giving of his time with me, but I just ignored many of those opportunities, which are lost forever. Parents can relate, but most teenagers can't see past their own noses. Trust me. I was one of those teenagers.

When I was fourteen, my buddy Gene Sowerwine and I were supposed to play eighteen holes with our fathers. Gene and I arrived at the course before Dad and Mr. Sowerwine. I don't recall, but I suspect both were still at work. Anyway, Gene and I tossed our golf bags on our shoulders and started our round as a twosome without them.

We were on the 2nd green when we noticed that Dad and Mr. Sowerwine had teed off and were a hole behind us. To this day, I don't know what goes through a young kid's mind. Gene and I thought if they really wanted to play the round with us, they'd speed up and catch us. We continued our round, even playing faster. While they also picked up their pace, we stayed a hole to a hole and a half in front of them, until the 11th tee box.

I greeted Dad with a big smile and said hello. Gene and I figured they'd be happy to join us. Think again.

Dad and Mr. Sowerwine barely acknowledged us. Dad looked at me and said, "The two of you are obviously enjoying yourselves as a twosome, so we will just play through and not interrupt your day." They teed off and played through in front of us.

Gene and I looked at each other. I am not sure I realized it immediately, but, boy, our decision not to wait for our dads was a bratty thing to do. I then realized the only reason Dad rushed from the office to get to the golf course was to spend time with me. And I know Mr. Sowerwine wanted to spend time with Gene too.

It is both amazing and appalling how I treated my dad that day, not only disregarding the time and effort he took to be with me but disrespecting him as well. Kids! Yes, I was a typical kid who thought only of himself and gave no thought to another person's interests, and, in my case, I intentionally and blatantly ignored Dad. That never happened again.

As each of my children hit the stage when he or she might have acted as I did on that course, I made sure to casually tell them that story, hoping they would listen and learn.

My five children—Jack III, Christina, Charlie, Casey, and Will—are each in different chapters of their lives. I have always tried to take the time to offer advice when asked or when I felt it was appropriate. I have also learned from them and love each one dearly.

The best way to describe the interaction I share with my children is *active*. Introduce each child to just about everything possible. Let them find their interests or passions, and support and encourage them to follow their dreams. I remember many times we spoke about the direction of their lives. I explained that if they were able to find something they loved to do in the classroom, on the athletic field, and in life, they would be amazed how good they would be at it. I can tell you that Dad found his passion in golf, and he felt as though he never worked a day in his life (at least on the golf course). A follow-up message I preach to my children is mostly about their effort. They know that whatever direction they choose in life, they need to give it their all.

Like you might imagine with five kids, I had to learn to listen to each one differently. As I've said, I wanted to take every opportunity to listen to them.

And, like Dad, I always learned from listening to my children.

CHAPTER 2

Attend Your Children's Games and Activities

Regardless of distance and destination, traveling for a career resonates with millions of dads and kids who might be separated almost every week. Dad traveled for a living too. He tried his best to be home as much as possible, and he also had a deal with Mom that he'd never be away from home for more than two weeks, which is longer than most families are separated by work travel.

My siblings—Michael, Nan, Steve, and Gary—and I were raised on sports, including golf, tennis, basketball, volleyball, football, and baseball. Nan went to Georgia on a volleyball scholarship. Steve attended Florida State on a football scholarship. Michael went to Georgia Tech on a golf scholarship. Gary, who dealt with the pressure of being "the Next Nicklaus" (as you will see in chapter three), went to Ohio State on a golf scholarship and later worked in the family business. (Gary rediscovered his love for the game and is now on the senior tour.) I was on a golf scholarship at North Carolina.

From Little League to college, Mom and Dad always made every effort to attend our games. Dad arranged his schedule to align with ours, sacrificing his time to be there for us.

At our home high school football games at the Benjamin School, Mom often worked the scoreboard, while Dad—though not technically a coach on the staff—slipped on a headset and helped coach our team from the roof of the nearby gymnasium. It was amazing when you think about it. Mom directed the household, and Dad focused on his profession. Yet here was Dad, one of the most famous athletes in the world, who did everything in his power to attend our games.

I can't imagine parents not wanting to cheer on and support their children. There were many times when Dad literally traveled across the country to attend our games. What I realized later—and appreciated even more—was that even though Dad had the means to be able to attend our games, he had to actively choose to be there. He could have easily just telephoned any of us kids from the road and asked about our games. Even now Dad (Peepaw) and Mom (Mimi) display that same commitment to their grandchildren. They always try to attend every event without fail, even if they must divide and conquer.

Dad made family his priority, and he has passed this trait on to us. I am so grateful. Dad missed only two games in the five years that Steve and I (we're only a year apart) played football in high school.

There are a few Friday nights I will never forget. One was when we played our football rival Glades Day School, near Lake Okeechobee in Central Florida. Dad was playing in the World Series of Golf in Akron, Ohio, but only agreed to compete if officials guaranteed him an early tee time Friday so he could make our game. As soon as he walked off the last green, he flew to Florida, and we awarded him a great game.

We won, and both Steve and I played well. Still dressed in the golf clothes he played in that day, Dad was so excited when he met us on the field. He hugged us, voiced his pride, slapped us on our butts, and then headed back to the airport for a return flight to Ohio. And it wasn't like the airport was around the block! The nearest airport was forty miles away, in our hometown of West Palm Beach.

In 1978 we played Florida A&M University Developmental Research School in the Class 1A state title game at Bragg Memorial Stadium in Tallahassee. Dad was playing in the Mexican Open in Mexico City, but he still made our game (we lost), gave us a hug when it was over, and jumped back on his plane to Mexico for the tournament. At least this time, the local airport was only a few minutes away from the stadium.

Another memorable Friday night was in my junior season (Steve was a sophomore) in a game against Frostproof, located in Polk County, Florida, in the state playoffs. I played tight end, and Steve started at wide receiver and safety. I had separated my shoulder in a game the previous week, so my playing time was limited. Steve, on defense, covered a deep pass and looked back over his shoulder. He never saw the base of the goal post and ran full speed into it. He immediately was knocked out cold, crumpled to the ground, and lay there motionless. The crowd went silent.

Dad and Mom were in the stands, and Dad had never come out on the field during a game. But this time, as the coaches ran to Steve, Dad was right on their heels. It looked bad, and everyone was concerned. Our offensive coordinator, Tom Mullins, was kneeling over Steve when Dad arrived, but thankfully Steve was okay. He eventually sat up, a little groggy and clearly seeing stars, and it was obvious he was going to be fine after a few minutes. Dad, the ultracompetitor and always dialed in, saw his opening to offer advice to the coaches after he made sure Steve was in one piece.

Dad grabbed Tom's elbow and said, "Frostproof's secondary is hanging way back on defense, and the middle of the field is wide open. It's been open all night." On our next offensive series, a recovered Steve caught a pass across the middle and scored a touchdown for our first lead of the game. Dad's smile stretched the width of the field. We won 7–6.

We've all heard the horror stories of overbearing parents or grandparents who scream at officials and embarrass their children and grandchildren. Dad was never that parent—and isn't that grandparent. I have never heard Dad, the fan, shout at an official in an angry or negative manner. Sportsmanship with Dad was always paramount. It's like that famous quote, "It's not whether you win or lose, it's how you play the game." The actual quote came from Grantland Rice's poem "Alumnus Football," in which he wrote, "For when the One Great Scorer comes to mark against your name, He writes—not that you won or lost—but how you played the Game."[1] Rice's words go well beyond sports. They touch on how we live our lives and the importance of putting things in perspective. Nobody was more competitive than Dad was on the golf course, but he also knew that decency, sportsmanship, integrity, and kindness mattered far more.

Some things are simply more important than the final score. Nobody knows that better than Dad. For every winner, there's a second-place finisher. Dad leads the PGA Tour with eighteen major wins. He also leads the PGA Tour with the most second-place finishes in majors with nineteen, seven of which came at the Open Championship. It was always important to Dad to be gracious in victory or defeat. But don't misunderstand me. Nobody wants to win more than my dad—other than maybe my mom!

Dad is all about winning, from his preparation to his drive to his goals. If it's not a competition, Dad loses interest very quickly. When Mom and Dad play backgammon or any board game, step back, because it's a competition. (I will speak more to their competitiveness later.) When we were younger, Dad, Steve, and I played golf, and the winner won a milkshake. If Dad won, we'd make him a milkshake at the house. If Steve or I won, Dad drove us to Dairy Queen for a milkshake. Even now, if we fish on a lazy Sunday afternoon, it immediately turns competitive. Who can catch the most fish? Who can catch the biggest fish?

Dad's number-one goal, though, is to support his children and grandchildren. Dad and Mom have traveled the country to watch grandson Nick O'Leary (Bill and Nan's son, and my nephew) play football. Nick played at Florida State, was drafted by the Buffalo Bills, and has been in the NFL since 2015. And no matter where the grandchildren are playing, Dad and Mom are almost always in the stands.

Of course, Dad's usually the most recognizable face in the stands when he attends games, and there's always a murmur when he arrives. It is also neat to see how Dad interacts with fans at games involving family members. He's laser focused on the game, but he's also always polite and friendly to everyone. I remember one of my son Charlie's high school lacrosse games, when the Benjamin School played Cooper City High School in

Fort Lauderdale during the state playoffs. Fans lined up four hundred deep to get Dad's autograph, and he signed every request after the game.

I am very quiet in the stands when I watch my children, even though my emotions are blowhorn-loud on the inside. I developed my approach with my kids from a lacrosse survey that I once read, which focused on what words were most appropriate to say to a child after a game. The survey noted you might say "Great play," which wouldn't register because the child might think otherwise. The survey also asked players what they thought was the most powerful comment they heard from their parents. The top answer was "I loved watching you play today." That was it. That really hit me, so much so that I changed the words I said to my children. I think all my kids have heard me say that after every game they played since. "I loved watching you play today." But I added an important caveat: "Did you have fun?"

I know from experience how difficult it is for a father to teach his children. After their games, they weren't ready to hear my critique on how well they played or didn't play. Win or lose, there is still too much adrenaline and emotions—or whatever it might be immediately after a game. My approach has been more quiet and humble. But make no mistake. I enjoy winning as much as anyone, including my father. I remain a fierce competitor. It is simply not something I wear on my sleeve.

I also don't think there was a standard message passed down from my father to me. Dad was a little more hands-on with me than I was with my children. I played catch with my kids, shot free throws, worked on whatever. When I say hands-on, I mean that Dad was more technical with me when I was young. For instance, after one of my basketball games, Dad might immediately have taken me to the free throw line to work on my form; after a golf event, he might work with me on my chipping.

I see Dad today, as a grandfather in his eighties, as an authority for me. Outside of God, he is the final word. I may analyze what he says, but what he says is close to the gospel because I have so much respect for his knowledge and his methods.

That wasn't always the case even though he was a great teacher. When I was younger, I had difficultly hearing instruction from Dad. I often put up a barrier when Dad tried to teach me how to do or not do something. Sometimes the timing of his instruction may have kept me from receiving it well. When he approached me at the right time, I was usually more receptive to his instruction.

I think I am more cognizant of that with my kids—again, maybe it goes back to Dad being more competitive than I am. Maybe my approach was different with my children because early on I realized I wasn't going to win eighty-two tournaments. I wasn't going to achieve the things Dad achieved. I wanted to make this about enjoying the journey. And that's what I chose to teach. Please don't get me wrong. I am not a fan of participation awards. In sports there are winners and losers, but winning in life is so much more important.

Dad has instilled in his children and grandchildren the drive to compete, improve, and strive to win in whatever we do, but he also believes that we often learn more from our defeats than our victories because those losses provide opportunities to improve and teach resilience and courage. A defeat simply highlights a need to work harder to prepare for the next battle.

Dad always stayed in the present too. And that was a

teaching lesson I tried to share with my kids—even under difficult circumstances.

Some of the greatest times I enjoyed as a parent were the times I watched them compete on the athletic fields. Of all the events we attended, my favorite is girls' high school volleyball. Cheering for Christie and Casey as they got competitive was the best. Watching my Jack, Charlie, and Will compete on the football and lacrosse fields is really special, as well. If I could have a simple message to share with any parent, it would be to embrace every moment. Your kids really do grow up so fast.

As you might expect, my children pursued very different things. Jack graduated from Florida State University and went to work for a developer in New York City. Christie also graduated from FSU and works for a real estate developer based in Palm Beach. Charlie, who graduated from Rutgers University and played lacrosse for RU, is a boat broker. Casey is my third graduate from FSU. She works for a sports marketing and entertainment group based in New York. Will is attending the University of North Carolina at Chapel Hill, my alma mater. He plays on the lacrosse team and was recently accepted into the Kenan-Flagler Business School.

When Will's lacrosse team was in the state semifinals his junior season at the Benjamin School, I sent him my customary pregame text: "Look forward to watching you play today, have fun." I also added, "I'll see you after the game." Will admitted he thought the second sentence was strange.

Dad attended that game, and as he always did, he waited for Will as he walked off the field. When Will saw Dad, he asked where I was. Dad explained that earlier in the day I had an unexpected but successful heart procedure (I had 85 percent blockage in one artery that required a stent) and that I hadn't wanted to interrupt his preparation and focus. I had wanted him to play to the best of his abilities without any distractions. That heart procedure also cost me the opportunity to attend Charlie's Senior Day at Rutgers. For me, it was everything to be present and support my kids. It killed me not to be there. In retrospect and with better perspective, it might have killed me to have been in attendance. On those two occasions, Mom and Dad were there in my place.

Dad won his last major in 1986 when, at age forty-six, he became the oldest winner in Masters history. By that time Dad had played in one hundred major championships, finishing in the top three nearly fifty times. My oldest son, Jack III, was born in 1990, so my kids didn't grow up watching Dad play professional golf. They knew him as Peepaw, their grandfather. Sure, they watched replays of Dad over the years, so they have had an opportunity to share in those moments that way—but only from watching old videos. Dad has also had his grandchildren caddie for him at the Wednesday par-3 tournament during Masters week.

One of Dad's most emotional moments happened in 2018, when his grandson GT (Gary's son) made a hole in one on the par-3 9th hole. Deservedly, GT's hole in one made ESPN's top-ten moments at the number-one spot. GT's playing group included Gary Player, Tom Watson, and Dad. It was the first time GT, at age fifteen, had caddied for his granddad at the Masters. What you need to know is that there is a tradition in the par-3 tournament during Masters week to let the caddies take the shot at the

9th hole. GT made the most of it since this was the first hole in one he ever made. After GT's shot, Curtis Strange turned and shouted to Dad, "Where does this rank on your Masters list?"

Without saying a word, my emotional dad pointed up one finger. It was number one on his list. It was a day scripted so well. Dad finished third that day, and GT, in his white caddie uniform, hits one shot—and it's a hole in one. Incredible!

Like Dad, I always made every effort to attend every single sports game, every art show, every awards ceremony, and every school performance of my children. I wanted them to see my face in the stands supporting them. I always tried to put my family first no matter how hectic my work schedule was at the time. I wanted to make sure I was the first person to give them a hug.

We all represent ourselves, but we also represent our last name, Nicklaus. We have our own responsibilities to carry on the Nicklaus legacy in the correct manner. A lot of people may think, *Oh, it's great having the last name of Nicklaus.* But with that last name comes a great responsibility. Yes, we all stub our toes from time to time. But I am very proud of my kids because I believe they walk through life understanding their actions will reflect not only on their father but also—the way I see it, and more importantly—on their grandfather. That is a big responsibility to have. I have carried it my entire life, and I am proud of my kids because they keep that in mind when they make decisions in life.

Their actions are a reflection on their Peepaw and Mimi.

Even though my dad traveled a great deal during his career, he always put his family first. While he faced a lot of pressures when he was traveling, Dad came home as much as possible to attend our games and events. We can all learn from that, especially those of us who travel for our jobs. Children, especially young ones, might not fully understand why parents have to be on the road for their work. They can feel ignored, slighted, even not cared for. Attending your children's events—baseball games, dance recitals, musical performances, or golf tournaments—serves as a reminder to your kids that nothing is more important to you than they are.

CHAPTER 3

Raise Each Child Differently

It's not unusual for a child at some stage of life to aspire to be in the same profession as his or her father, whether he be a carpenter, firefighter, business executive—or even a professional golfer. Though Dad never pushed me or any of my siblings into golf, we all migrated to it. Again, with the best seat in the house and the opportunity to learn from the best golfer of all time, it would seem to make great sense.

But it was accompanied by challenges.

When I played golf professionally for nearly four years in the late 1980s, I can't tell you how many times I heard people say under their breath, "He will never be as good as his dad. He will never win as many tournaments as his dad."

Really?

News alert, people.

I never said this but wanted to: "I am trying to win my *first* professional golf tournament, not my eightieth!"

Being Jack Nicklaus II was probably toughest for me as a teenager. Like most teenagers, I couldn't see past my nose. When

I went to the University of North Carolina to play golf in the early 1980s, I continued to learn about myself. I was always proud to be Dad's son, but I also wanted to be recognized for what I accomplished. It was a daily process and a continual challenge.

When I was at UNC, I rarely said my last name when I met people for the first time. I often said, "Hi, I'm Jack," as opposed to, "Hi, I'm Jack Nicklaus." I didn't want people to immediately go, "Oh, there's Jack Nicklaus's son." My good friend Scott Stankavage, who was a quarterback on the Tar Heels football team, picked up on what I was doing and asked why I didn't reveal my last name. I wanted people to see who I was before they identified me as Jack Nicklaus's son. I wanted them to talk to me as a normal person before they figured it out.

Because invariably, people have always treated me differently as Jack Nicklaus II.

I will say this though: Not everyone has recognized Dad! I was with him in Asia when a woman on the elevator asked Dad, "Do you know who you are? Do you know who you are?" Dad smiled and said, "I think so." The woman was adamant. "Do you know who you are? You are Arnold Palmer!"

Dad laughed and said, "No, I'm Jack Nicklaus."

She shook her head back and forth, walked from the elevator, and said, "No, you are Arnold Palmer."

When I was playing in high school, Dad told me he was more interested in me liking the game of golf than having great golf fundamentals.

I asked him why, and Dad explained: "I know it will be tough on you at times, but I would rather you enjoy the game than somehow think you should match my records." As a result, Dad didn't push me on fundamentals. He just wanted me to have fun.

And that worked for me.

Kids don't come with an instruction manual. Parents learn as they go. Dad took a much different approach with my younger brother Gary, ordained "the Next Nicklaus" on the cover of the March 11, 1985, issue of *Sports Illustrated*. He was sixteen years old.

Dad was harder on Gary when it came to golf fundamentals. As a result, Gary is great fundamentally and is now playing on the PGA Champions Tour. Gary is a good player, a far better player than I am. His short game was always so good. I always loved his confidence too.

I have never forgotten this moment, and it still makes me laugh. It was Christmas 1980, and I was a freshman at North Carolina. South Florida is a great place in the winter to work on your golf game, so I returned home to North Palm Beach for the Christmas break. Two of my UNC teammates visited, and one afternoon we played golf at Frenchman's Creek in Palm Beach Gardens. We had a fivesome—Dad, my two college teammates, eleven-year-old Gary, and me.

We were on the 9th hole, which had water in front of the green, and Gary hit his approach shot over the green and into the bunker. His ball was on a slight downward slope in the sand. There was about eight feet of Bermuda grass rough between the bunker and the green, which sloped away from Gary. The pin was tucked in the back of the green, so Gary had very little green to work with from the bunker. There was also a lake staring at Gary, should he overhit his bunker shot. It was a very difficult shot for a golfer of any age, let alone one who was eleven.

Gary stepped into the bunker with a confident, cute smile. Actually, it was an annoying little smile to his older brother but, nonetheless, a priceless little smile. Gary settled his feet in the sand, and just before he began his back swing, he paused, looked up, and made sure he had everyone's attention. Gary confidently announced, "Just so you all know, they call *me* the king from here." My teammates and I cracked up with laughter. Dad laughed too, and asked, "What did you say?" I think Dad just wanted to hear Gary say it again.

Gary said with a big smile, "Yes. They call me the king."

Gary settled into his stance and took a slow, beautifully rhythmic swing back and through the ball. Unfortunately Gary peeked a little too early and lifted his head. His club hit the ball before the sand. We all heard that awful sound of the leading edge of the clubface slapping the center of the golf ball. The ball rose as it sailed past the flag stick, over the green, and into the middle of the lake. God love Gary, it was so funny. Everyone howled. That Christmas break Gary earned the nickname "the king."

When *Sports Illustrated* named Gary the "Heir to the Bear," the magazine touted that "At 16, Gary Nicklaus is a golfer of immense promise, with a style uncannily like that of his proud and watchful papa, the great Jack." The magazine's cover featured Gary, in white shorts and a light garnet shirt, following through his swing, an iron in his grip and a pile of white golf balls waiting at his feet behind him. A small photograph of Dad, from the chest up in his follow through, was inserted on the cover with the caption "Here's Jack's son Gary. He's only 16, but already he can beat the old man (sometimes)."[1]

The *SI* reporter Barry McDermott wrote, "Maybe it's true what people are saying: The kid can inherit the old man's business." He noted in the article, "In some ways Gary faces a tougher course than do other boys with similar ability. Golfing talent doesn't seem to travel well from generation to generation."[2]

Gary was that good. He had all the potential to be a world beater. At age eleven, he broke 80. At thirteen, as the youngest player ever in a Palm Beach County men's tournament, he tied for the title in the first flight—and beat me by more than twenty strokes even though I was already at UNC. He beat Dad for the first time when he was fifteen.

Some might enjoy being on the cover of a national magazine so much that they'd immediately have it framed. Not so for Gary, who ran from golf for the next two years after that cover. Dad wasn't happy with *Sports Illustrated* for their decision to write the story, mostly because of the way it impacted Gary. There again is the pressure of the Nicklaus name.

Gary disliked golf because of the limelight that was focused on him, mainly from that article. He went through a time when he did not like golf. Yes, he still played and competed in golf events and performed well enough to earn that scholarship at

Ohio State. But Gary did not have a love for the game until later in college as an all-American for the Buckeyes.

Gary turned professional in 1991, but he failed to earn his PGA card. He mainly played overseas and on mini-tours. Gary eventually recommitted himself to golf and was one shot away from being a mainstay on the PGA Tour, which I'll explain.

Gary went through qualifying school and made the PGA Tour in 2000. He survived what many longtime golf professionals will tell you is the most difficult test in golf. Gary worked out, ate correctly, and was dialed in.

In April of that same year, Gary finished second to Phil Mickelson in the BellSouth Classic in Atlanta. Gary and Phil were tied for the fifty-four-hole lead, but heavy rains on the final day left some of the greens unplayable for the final eighteen holes. Tour officials canceled the final round and called for a sudden-death playoff to determine a champion. On the first playoff hole, a par-3, Gary's tee shot landed in the bunker while Phil's hit the green, where he sank his birdie putt to win the tourney.

Phil did what any golfer should do—he earned the win. We can look back and wonder, *What if?* That win would have been a difference-maker for Gary. I am not talking about the winner's check. I am talking about the two-year exemption to play on the PGA Tour that accompanies a tour win. It also would have improved his confidence. There will always be pressure on golfers to perform and win again. It is a different program because winning breeds winning. We all have our doubts. But a win would have legitimized Gary. He would have belonged. He would not have been riding on Dad's coattails.

Had Gary gotten a win under his belt in Atlanta, he would have been a regular on the PGA Tour. The Champions tour is for those golfers fifty years and older who had previous PGA Tour membership. Gary just needs that one break to prove in his own mind that he belongs. I hope it happens soon, as the Champions tour is a narrow window.

Obviously Dad's investment in Gary's fundamentals worked—just as much as his choice to make sure I enjoyed the game worked too. That was the only way I could grind out what would become my four-year professional golf career.

I remember when I played in the Southern Open, which was a golf tournament on the PGA Tour from 1970 to 2002. It was a Friday evening, and I had missed the cut (again). I was in the locker room, and most everyone had left the property. I had just tipped the locker room attendant and thanked him for looking after me during my week in Columbus, Georgia. And it was a full week. You went at it all day—warmups, competition, post-round practice, press interviews, interacting with the gallery, and sponsor commitments.

As usual, I had the weekend off. If I remember correctly, the Southern Open was my tenth consecutive week on the road. I was married, and being on the road that long was a challenge. I was about to leave the locker room when I noticed a huge Rubbermaid cooler in the middle of the room filled with ice and beer. I am not a big beer drinker. Honestly, I don't think I had a beer or any alcohol during that ten-week stretch. I was a nerd when it came to drinking alcohol while I was trying to get better on the golf course. I wanted to do everything I could to have a chance at success.

I remember being exhausted, mentally and physically. The locker room attendant looked at me and said, "Go ahead, have a beer. They're ice cold." They looked good, so I said, "What the heck?" I dug in the cooler, pulled out a Bud Light, and popped the top. As I walked from the locker room, two fans, probably in their forties or fifties, strolled by me. They didn't break stride as they looked at me and then to each other. "Unbelievable," one of them said. "You would never see his father have a beer."

I already knew I had a spotlight on me. That comment was confirmation that people were going to judge me regardless. But there came a point when I finally figured out I wasn't going to play the game at the elite level needed to make a living.

After I graduated from UNC in 1985, I bounced around the world for those four seasons competing in professional tours in Canada, Australia, Asia, and Europe. It was so difficult financially—I barely made any money—that I watched where every penny and dime went. One year I entered the Palm Coast Tournament in Australia, where, on the 18th hole on a Friday night, I had about a foot-and-a-half putt that I thought was going to allow me to make the cut by one shot . . . and make a little money. I remember shaking like a leaf as I stood over that putt, trying to control my nerves and my emotions. I don't know how I made the putt, but it went in. Sadly, I still missed the cut because I had miscalculated the cut line—and made no money.

Later that night I thought to myself, *What am I doing? I am out here just trying to make a cut?* Whether for me or for Dad or for the people who expected me to play well, I put so much pressure on myself to perform. I didn't play much longer after that tournament. Lingering ill health from a tick bite and from a rib injury made the decision easier.

It was time to chase other goals, specifically in Dad's golf design company.

I have tried to raise my five children in the same manner that my parents raised me and Gary—differently. I have had to call audibles as I have raised them, and that's okay. Like any parent, I've taken cues from understanding how each child is wired. You can't use a cookie-cutter approach because it will drive you crazy. When my son Jack first started to play football at age eight, he couldn't run or catch the ball. I was like, "Come on, Jack, let's go. Catch the ball."

Fast-forward a couple of years. I sat in the same stands watching him run and catch the football on the field where I had played. He looked great. I overheard a few parents shouting some of the same things at their boys that I had shouted at Jack a few years earlier. I asked, "Is that your firstborn son?" They said, "Yes, how did you know?" I laughed and said, "Let me tell you a story."

I told them their son would be okay; they just needed to give him time. But not to necessarily apply that lesson to the next child because each child is an entirely different person.

CHAPTER 4

Keep Teaching—Even If Your Child Doesn't Want to Learn

It is a difficult dynamic for a father and son to always communicate on a calm and rational level. I know from my childhood—and even today—that it is a challenge to listen and immediately value a father's advice, regardless of his qualifications. Hopefully, this embarrassing story will provide some comfort and encouragement to fathers to be more patient.

The year was 1973. I was eleven and playing in the Columbus District Golf Tournament. I was having a tough day on the course (imagine that!), and I had missed another short putt. I was upset as I walked off the green, and Dad, who had been following me the entire round, offered his two cents as we walked to the next tee.

To put this story in perspective, Dad had won two of the four majors the year before. He won the Masters and the U.S. Open by three shots each in wire-to-wire fashion. Many believed Dad had a good chance to become only the second golfer since Bobby Jones in 1930 to complete the Grand Slam—winning golf's four major championships in the same calendar year. Though he didn't win the Grand Slam, Dad had an incredible year in '72. He competed in twenty worldwide events, winning seven, placing second in four of them, and registering fifteen top-ten finishes.

But in that Columbus District Golf Tournament, I wasn't having the best of days on the greens, and Dad's advice irritated me even further. My reaction was clearly etched across my face. A gentleman standing nearby asked, "What did your dad say?"

I replied, "He told me to keep my head still when I putt." For emphasis, I added, "He knows *nothing* about golf!"

There you have it.

The Golden Bear—the winner of 117 professional tournaments in his career—knows nothing about golf. I am embarrassed to this day about my reaction and response. Still, I can also laugh about it because I know how absurd it must have sounded. "He knows *nothing* about golf."

What in the world was I thinking? I can answer my own question.

I wasn't thinking.

I truly did not understand the big picture as a kid. I can vividly remember getting upset just about every time I hit a golf shot that was anything less than really good. I pouted and was grumpy and emotional. Depending on my age, it was important to me to break 80 or to break 90. I was such a pain in the butt! I know Dad was constantly trying to help me with my golf swing and how to think my way around a golf course. But there were times when I just tuned him out.

So, for all the dads out there, be patient with your kids. For all the kids out there, I know it's hard to believe that your dad probably knows just a little more than you're giving him credit for. Heck, it was difficult for me to accept advice not only from Dad but even from other professionals as I gained more experience. However, I also learned that advice and how you react to it can go both ways.

I played in the Pebble Beach Pro-Am at the Cypress Point Club in California as an amateur at age nineteen. My partner was Tim Simpson, who is a few years older than I am and turned professional three years earlier. Tim played at the University of Georgia and won four PGA titles during his career. At one point, Tim was described by Dad and others as one of the best ball strikers in the game.

I was a confident, stubborn teenager and a freshman at UNC when I was partnered with Tim. We played well in the Pro-Am and were close to the lead. On the 9th tee, I pulled out a 3-wood from my bag. I thought it was the perfect club selection because the 9th hole is the shortest par-4 on the course at 289 yards and reachable from the tee. I had every intention to drive the green.

Tim stopped me and said, "You need to lay up." I told Tim, "I'm feeling it." I believed I could knock my drive on the green and have an opportunity at an eagle. If I missed the green and landed in a bunker, I knew it was a simple sand shot to where the pin was located.

Tim literally pulled the 3-wood from my hands and handed me the 4-iron from my bag. I insisted the 4-iron was the wrong club to use since the distance I hit that club would have left me in the narrowest part of the fairway, between sand and rough. Tim was frustrated and said, "Hit the 4-iron. I've played this game a lot longer than you."

I hit the 4-iron and, unfortunately, pulled it left into a fairway sand trap—probably the worst line from the pin, which was in the back of the green, about sixty-five yards away. I hit my bunker shot thin, and the ball landed over the green. It was a near-impossible chip shot, and I left the ball twenty feet from the cup. I missed the putt and bogeyed the hole. In the meantime, Tim hit his drive into the rough and double-bogeyed. In the span of one hole, we went from near the top of the leaderboard to potentially missing the cut.

That wasn't the only damage done. Tim was upset at how I handled the exchange and didn't acknowledge me at the end of the round. No handshake, no nothing. He just stormed off. As it turned out, we made the cut and advanced in the tournament. I saw Tim on the range the following day and walked over to say hello. Again, he barely acknowledged me. We met on the 1st tee for our round and not much was said between us. The first few holes were really uncomfortable. However, we both eventually loosened up and enjoyed the rest of our round. I think we both realized we had been acting like children.

But I'm not the only Nicklaus boy who had trouble accepting advice.

I had turned pro and played in the Pebble Beach Pro-Am with my good friend John Purcell. Dad was teamed with my younger brother Steve. We were in the 10th fairway when Dad, all smiles and laughing, walked toward me. Dad said, "I have to share something with you. Have you noticed that Steve hasn't said a word to me the last four holes?" I answered, "No. Why?" Dad explained that on the 6th hole, Steve missed the fairway and hit his drive into the Pacific Ocean. Making matters worse, Dad also missed a five-foot birdie putt on the same hole.

Dad said, "Steve is really pissed at me."

Apparently Steve thought Dad should have made the putt, alleviating the damage Steve's mistake had cost the team. "Does he really think I missed that putt on purpose?" Dad asked, barely finishing the sentence because he was laughing so hard. But Dad drained a ten-foot birdie putt on the 10th hole, so all was forgiven, and Steve finally started to talk to Dad again.

Dad used that moment to teach both of us the importance of moving on after setbacks. We all experience setbacks either in life or on the golf course, but we can't let them define us. We can learn from our missteps, but we also need to know when to move on from them and not obsess and get angry over our mistakes and frustrations.

I learned that lesson from another golfer—thanks, of course, to Dad.

It was early in my professional career, and I caddied for Dad at Muirfield Village in his Memorial Tournament. It was the Wednesday shoot-out, an entertaining tournament-style event where one golfer is eliminated on each of ten holes by having the highest score. It was a lot of fun, and the crowd was engaged and enjoying it. The tournament came down to two players: Dad and Peter Jacobson, who won seven events on the PGA Tour and is a commentator on the Golf Channel and NBC.

Despite the light mood, I was really focused and dialed in to help Dad. On the 9th tee, Peter asked me, "Jackie, how is your golf game?" I replied, "Peter, I'm hitting the ball really well, but, gosh, I'm not putting very well." Peter looked at me and said sternly, "I don't want to ever hear you say that to me again, that you are not putting well."

As we walked down the fairway, Peter explained to me what he meant. "Your mind is like a computer," he said. "It only knows what you tell it. And if you keep telling yourself you are a bad putter, you are going to be a bad putter." Peter told me I had to figure out a way to convince myself that I was putting well. He said I had to start between my ears before I worried about how I was holding the club.

We walked another fifty yards down the fairway, where Dad's and Peter's tee shots were next to each other. Dad hit his approach shot to the middle of the green as Peter pulled an 8-iron from his bag. Dad, Peter, and all golfers have their own pre-shot routine—set your stance, waggle your club, look at the target, and go. Peter was near the end of his pre-shot routine, his club positioned behind the ball, and he appeared ready to swing.

I was ten feet away, holding Dad's golf bag, when Peter lifted his head and peered at me, expressionless. He asked, "Jackie, do you know what club I'm hitting?"

I said, "No sir."

He said, "I'm hitting an 8-iron. Ask me what kind of an 8-iron player I am."

I obliged. "What kind of an 8-iron player are you?"

A smile spread across Peter's face as he answered, "I am the best 8-iron player on this planet."

Peter looked back down at the ball, swung, and his approach shot landed near the pin and rolled within six inches of the cup. Peter grinned and slapped a high-five with me as we walked down the fairway. I looked at Dad and said, "Sorry, Dad!" That is a perfect example of how much fun players can have out there while in competition. And even though I was caddying for Dad, I appreciated that Peter took the time to offer that advice.

Maybe it was a little easier for me to accept the lesson from Peter because I knew *he* knew something about golf. As a father, I have had to learn to make sure the messages I hope my children are receiving come from a handful of different voices and experiences. It took me years to figure out that Dad had been doing that too. But he kept teaching even if I wasn't listening.

We all can learn from Dad's example here. Our children often seem to be tuning us out. They can give in to their anger the way Steve and I did out on the golf course. They can be distracted by all the bells and whistles that are part of modern life: video games, social media, sports, activities, schoolwork, their social lives, and everything else under the sun. Dad never gave up when it came to teaching his children, despite the pushback we often gave him. You shouldn't either.

CHAPTER 5

Act Like a Champion

In both actions and words, Dad has had a great ability to see the bigger picture throughout his life and career. He has always understood how things would affect him, the people around him, and his competitors.

I believe that capacity has helped define Dad as a champion.

"The Concession" is widely regarded as one of the greatest gestures of sportsmanship ever witnessed in golf. Dad's act of generosity on the final day of the 1969 Ryder Cup lives on to this day. During an interview with *Golfweek* in 2019, Dad laughed and said, "There's been a lot of mileage out of just a two-foot putt."[1]

The Ryder Cup has often been described as the best event in sports. Today the biennial matches pit twelve of the United States' best golfers against twelve of Europe's best and are usually packed with incredible drama and energy.

For nearly a century, as the venue alternates between continents, fans make the Ryder Cup the event it is. Cheers, chants, and songs can be heard across the course. It's not the traditional, reserved golf-clap event that players are accustomed to in the States. Many players from both sides have said standing on the 1st tee of a Ryder Cup match has been one of the most nervous moments of their professional lives.

Dad played in six Ryder Cups during his career from 1969 to 1981. He played twenty-eight matches and had an overall record of sixteen wins, eight losses, and three halves (ties for the match). Dad went 4–0 in his last Ryder Cup appearance as a player in 1981, when the United States easily beat Europe 18.5 to 9.5. Dad also captained the 1983 and 1987 USA teams, finishing 1–1.

In 1969 the competition was strictly between the United States' and Great Britain's best. Dad was a Ryder Cup rookie, and the United States was coming off five consecutive wins. That year the tournament was played at the Royal Birkdale Golf Club in Southport, England. With thirty-one of the thirty-two matches completed, the two teams were tied at fifteen and a half apiece. So the winner of the Ryder Cup came down to the event's final match, between Dad and England's Tony Jacklin, who was a European hero because he had just won the Open Championship. He was the first player from Great Britain or Ireland to win a major since Max Faulkner won the Open Championship in 1951. Both were in their prime. Dad was twenty-nine, and Tony was twenty-five.

At the par-5 17th, Tony drained a thirty-five-foot eagle putt to square the match with Dad. Imagine the drama. After every match had been played, it was down to one hole. The stakes couldn't have been higher. As a long par-4, the 18th is considered an excellent finishing hole. Both players were on the green in two. And the tension could be felt by everyone. Tony had a thirty-foot putt for a birdie, and Dad had a fifteen-footer. Both players missed their putts. Tony left himself with a two-footer for par, while Dad sent his birdie putt four-and-a-half feet by the cup.

Dad, up first, needed his par putt to secure the Ryder Cup for the Americans. As reigning champions, the Americans would retain the cup if the match ended in a tie. Dad lined up his putt and drained it. And in the next moment, he proved he was a champion.

If Tony missed his two-footer, the United States would have won outright and England's hero would have had his image damaged. Instead of forcing Tony in that moment, Dad bent over and picked up Tony's ball marker. He walked over and shook Tony's hand. Dad had conceded Tony's putt, and it ensured their individual match and the overall match ended in a 16–16 tie. The two walked off with their arms wrapped around each other.

A few of his Ryder Cup teammates questioned Dad's decision. Team captain Sam Snead was not happy. "All the boys thought it was ridiculous to give him that putt," Snead told the media later. "We went over there to win, not to be good ol' boys."[2] Dad has repeatedly said over the years that his decision was about more than winning. Dad also believed Jacklin would have easily made his putt for the tie. However, Dad also knew what Tony meant to British golf—he couldn't walk down a street without being recognized. Dad thought if Tony somehow missed the putt, he would have been criticized forever. Dad decided in those few precious seconds not to give Tony an opportunity to miss.

I believe this gesture, which came to be known as the Concession, defines Dad. In a 2004 interview with ESPN, Tony reaffirmed my belief and talked about Dad's mindset:

"Jack always saw the big picture. That was the whole thing, really. That was his forte, all through his life," Jacklin said. "In a pressure situation, he would always think clearer than the next guy. That's why he came out on top in those pressure situations. He knew if he could get into the final group on Sunday in a major, he would be thinking better than his adversary.

"There it was the same thing. God only knows what he must have been thinking. All of a sudden, he's got a 4½-footer to make, and if he misses, his team loses the match. And then, in a split second, he holes the putt, and he's picking his ball out of the cup, and he picks my marker up at the same time. So he's run it all through his mind. He must have. But it was a spontaneous gesture," he added.[3]

While the Concession was always one of Dad's proudest golf moments, it also shows what it means to act like a champion by seeing beyond the moment that has everyone else fixated. Dad and Tony were so linked by this moment in golf history that a few years ago they were asked to design a golf course in Bradenton, Florida. Appropriately, the course is called the Concession.

Another spontaneous gesture from Dad that positively impacted a competitor came in 1980, when he won the U.S. Open at Baltusrol Golf Club in Springfield, New Jersey, two strokes in front of runner-up Isao Aoki of Japan. It was Dad's fourth U.S. Open title, which tied the record held by Willie Anderson, Bobby Jones, and Ben Hogan. Dad also set a tournament scoring record of 272 (8-under par) to break the record of 275 he set eleven years earlier on the same course. He birdied the last two holes to ensure the course record and took home a $50,000 bonus for the feat. The big check was offered by a national magazine to any player who could better the 275 four-day score Dad had previously set.

Again, this was another situation in which Dad was aware of the big picture. On the 18th green, both Dad and Isao were lining up birdie putts. Dad had a ten-footer, Isao's was a five-footer. Because Dad had the longer putt, he went first. He drained it and sealed the victory. The crowd erupted and started to storm the green in celebration. Dad immediately raised his arms and gestured for the fans to stay back because he realized how vital the putt was to Isao. While Isao couldn't beat Dad with a birdie, he was in line to earn the same $50,000 bonus for shooting below the 275 mark too. Isao made the putt and pocketed the bonus check.

As I had the chance to talk to him about these kinds of decisions over the years, the power of the lessons became clearer to me. Too often we find ourselves myopically focused on our situation in our moment—the me, me, me effect—forgetting how others will be impacted by the way we conduct ourselves. Dad showed me in that instant why he is a champion. He always thought of others.

Make no mistake, Dad wanted to be sure I understood that acting like a champion was about the way you carried yourself not just on the golf course but also in life. It's the way you project yourself to others, the belief you have in yourself, and the discipline you show in moments both good and bad. This was a life lesson. If you live your life as a champion, you could handle the criticism and the praise without being affected by either.

While I was writing this book, Dad shared a story I had never heard before, of a time when he was more concerned about the bigger picture than his own wallet. In the 1971 Atlanta Open, Dad lost to Gardner Dickinson in a sudden-death playoff. On that final hole, Gardner made his putt. Dad lined up and missed his, making Gardner the champion. Dad said that as he approached his ball, he realized that Gardner had been struggling for the previous two years and needed the win.

Dad made a point to say he didn't intentionally miss the putt, but he didn't go through his full routine of lining it up. In his entire career he can point to that as the one shot he took without winning in mind. Later in the evening he added that he did have a slight twinge of regret. But when he thought of the smile on Gardner's face, the regret went away.

The incredible thing about Dad is that he had this mindset even as a sixteen-year-old playing in the 1956 Ohio Open, paired with an older pro. When I met this man years later, he told me how nervous he was playing in that tournament. But my dad, he said, treated this enormous moment as just another day on the golf course, bouncing around the course in excitement without a care in the world. At one point on the back nine, the pro said Dad put his arm around him and said, "Hey, we make a couple birdies, we may just win this thing." Again, he said Dad, even as a teenager, knew how to keep the game in perspective, avoiding the anxiety that was affecting him and other players. The old club pro couldn't believe how well Dad handled the pressure at a young age.

Imagine, it was only six years earlier that Dad had played his first round of golf. He always makes a point to remind me and so many other people who look to him for advice that no matter how old you are, you need to act like a champion—and that often comes through in the way you carry yourself.

As I was getting better at golf, Dad wanted to make sure I was as driven to act like a champion as I was driven to become one.

In 1985 Dad opened the Bear Golf Course in Grand Traverse, Michigan. I had graduated from North Carolina a few months earlier and was coming off a tournament win at the North and South Amateur. The Bear is a difficult course, and the conditions weren't great on the day it opened, a day with a lot of wind. Because it was the celebration of the course's opening, a large crowd was in attendance, and many other golfers had showed up to play the course.

I wasn't playing very well, and, being an emotional twenty-three-year-old, it showed. I pouted, was upset, and hung my head throughout my round. Even though Dad was busy entertaining others, he spotted my frustration and asked, "What's with you?"

"Ahh, I'm playing bad," I said.

"You know what? What you are doing out here is embarrassing yourself. And you are embarrassing me too. You are a champion. You just won the North and South a few months ago. Why don't you represent that tournament, yourself, and me and play and act like a champion?"

While I shared the last name Nicklaus, people also saw me as the winner of a significant golf tournament. Although this message didn't necessarily settle in that day, in the moment I knew Dad was right. I had to concentrate on my behavior and act like a champion. I had never thought of it that way. I thought,

Hey, I won a tournament. No big deal. But if I was having a bad day on the course, I believed I could still act like a brat. It's understandable to be frustrated or angry. That's part of being a competitor. However, it takes great responsibility to act like a winner, to set an example, to think and live like a champion under any circumstance.

Dad often let us kids play golf with him before tournaments. In 1972 I was eleven years old when we played at Spyglass Hill Golf Course in Pebble Beach, California. It was the first hole—a 595-yard, par-5—and Dad said I moaned about my shots all the way down the fairway. By the time we reached the green, Dad had heard enough. He made me pick up my golf ball and bag, and we walked the five-hundred-plus yards back to the clubhouse!

I don't know how Dad put up with me on the course. I really don't. I once ripped my golf bag when I threw my club at it in a fit of anger after a bad shot. Dad warned he never wanted to see me do that again.

Grandpa taught Dad a similar lesson when Dad was eleven. Dad hit a fairway shot into the bunker near the green on the 15th hole at Scioto Country Club in Columbus. Upset, Dad threw his club, and it nearly landed in the bunker too. Grandpa told Dad if he ever saw that behavior again, it would be the last time he'd play golf. Grandpa made Dad pick up his club and ball, and they walked to the clubhouse. Same message, but at least Dad got fourteen holes in.

When my children were of similar age and I saw them acting the same way I did, on the golf course or playing other sports, I'd say to myself, *Jeez, the apple doesn't fall far from the tree*—and I'd have a quick "correct" with them.

Looking back over the generations, I've realized these lessons do not come naturally. Each generation has to take what they have learned and pass that knowledge and wisdom down to their children. Having learned all of those important lessons from Grandpa, Dad taught them to me. I in turn have taught them to my children, who will do the same with their children. Whether on the golf course or around the kitchen table, we always find those teachable moments and hand down what we learned many years before.

Starting in the 1960s, Arnold Palmer, Gary Player, and Dad were known as the "Big Three." The moniker was given to them by Mark McCormack, their shared manager, and they certainly had champion DNA. In 1962 the three of them won all four of the year's majors. In the 1960s the trio won seven of ten PGA Tour money titles and seventeen of the decade's forty majors.

Arnold arrived on the scene in 1955 and became known as the King, and his charisma matched his talents. Gary, born in South Africa, became an international golf star and was nicknamed the "Black Knight" because he always wore black clothes on the course to make him feel stronger. While their agent wanted it to be about the Big Three, most American golf fans saw it as a two-man show. And that rivalry was Palmer-Nicklaus.

Dad has said in interviews that the rivalry began in 1958, when he was an eighteen-year-old amateur. Dad was invited to participate in an event that honored professional golfer Dow

Finsterwald, who had just won the 1958 PGA Championship. Dad out-drove Arnold in a ball-striking contest and didn't hesitate to remind him of it—to which Arnold responded, "I shot a 63 that day, and you were four strokes behind." The two never hesitated to talk trash to each other, to give each other the needle. They both could give it and take it.

In those early days, Arnold was always the crowd favorite while Dad had to work so hard to gain the public's embrace. Dad famously beat Arnold in a playoff to win the 1962 U.S. Open at Oakmont—in Arnold's backyard—and was a runner-up to Arnold six times, including the 1960 U.S. Open.

Arnold and Dad agreed on one important thing—they always had each other's back. They were fierce competitors in golf and business but were always friends. I think as they got older, they admired each other more and more. If you looked for charisma, Arnold was your guy. If you looked for a role model, Dad was your guy.

The Big Three always played like champions—carrying themselves well and seldom collapsing during the stretch run of a tournament—which led to a lesson that Gary Player taught me.

While Greg Norman won eighty-nine titles worldwide and was inducted into the World Golf Hall of Fame in 2001, his collapse in the 1996 Masters was tough to watch. Greg led the first three rounds and carried a six-stroke advantage into the final round. However, he shot a 78 and lost by five strokes to Nick Faldo. I caddied for Dad at that tournament, and he started well, shooting a 70–73 in the first two rounds and finishing 9 over par.

As we flew from Augusta to Palm Beach following the tournament, Gary looked at me and said, "Jackie, what you saw today with Greg Norman, you never saw your father, Arnold, or myself do."

"What do you mean, Gary?" I asked.

"Your father, Arnold, and myself, we beat each other. We work hard, and we might play better than the other. And we will win; we will beat the other," Gary said. "But we never 'lost' a golf tournament. Today you watched Greg Norman *lose* a golf tournament."

This says a lot about the mindset of the Big Three. They rarely beat themselves. They honestly felt they never "lost" an event. They may have gotten outplayed and acknowledged it, but they never choked or made excuses. Any of them could have easily pointed to bad luck, complained, or made excuses. But they never did.

My father was more focused on acting like a champion than becoming one.

Dad has always believed that if you prepare, work hard, and do your best—playing within yourself and not making silly decisions—you don't lose. If your opponent plays better than you, you get beat—you don't lose. But if you don't prepare, play like a dog because you aren't ready, or take silly chances, you deserve to get beat. It's that simple.

Dad promised that great champions have the ability to do the right thing and take responsibility for what happens next. I have tried to teach my children that they might not immediately win people over. But if they follow Dad's example and consistently make good decisions, people eventually understand what you are about as a person, what's in your soul.

Whether you win or lose, always accept the final outcome with dignity and respect for your opponent. This lesson can be applied to so many aspects of life—work, relationships, and other areas. If you carry yourself like a champion and act like a champion throughout your life, you will inevitably pull positive energy and outcomes into your life.

I have told my children that you don't want to be remembered by what you did on the field. You want to be remembered by how you lived your life. You want to be remembered for living like a champion.

CHAPTER 6

See the Best in Others

Mom has said it for years and years, and I agree: Dad is trusting and forgiving to a fault. But he would argue the reason is because we should all look for the best in others first.

If a person's makeup is 80 percent good and 20 percent bad, Dad always focused on the good. Since we are talking in percentages, I guarantee Dad ignored the bad in people 100 percent of the time. Even though Dad's forgiving nature has cost him a lot of money—there have been times bad business deals have brought Dad to his knees—he's always had the ability to get back on his feet and recover.

I am going to admit this is a lesson from my father I have always struggled with. I am more suspicious of others than he is. I wish I weren't, but I am. It might be because I have focused more on the times when Dad was hurt or burned in a business deal than the many times his judgment was spot-on. Maybe I see conspiracies more than I should. I have tried to caution Dad when, for example, I didn't think a particular person was working in his best interests. Dad always gave that person a second chance. Maybe even a third.

Dad has admitted to both Mom and me that he's probably too trusting.

Regardless of my opinion, Dad's 80-20 rule has certainly worked. He's not only one of the greatest golfers ever, but he's also a very successful businessman off the course. Dad's Golden Bear brand has a global reach that includes golf course design, the development of golf and real estate communities, and the marketing and licensing of lifestyle products. Dad started licensing products in 1962 and formed the company eight years later, but when he stepped away from the day-to-day operations of Nicklaus Companies in 2018, that freed him up to focus more on his charity work and children's health care.

But don't be mistaken. Dad's company website speaks about who Dad is as a person, which is also reflected in the company's mission:

> For 50 years, the mission of Nicklaus Companies has been to enhance the golf experience and to deliver quality branded products and services on a global basis that mirror the high standards established in the career and life of its Founder, Jack Nicklaus.[1]

In 2007 Dad partnered with Howard Milstein to help further grow the company and realize the full potential of its branded businesses. Products include golf clothing, headwear, memorabilia, books, videos, and more. Nicklaus brands have also partnered with industry leaders, from Perry Ellis International (the largest manufacturer of golf apparel) to Toro (a golf course equipment and irrigation company).

Howard has served as executive chairman of the Nicklaus Companies since 2018, and he also sits on the board of the Nicklaus Children's Health Care Foundation. Howard is also the chairman, president, and CEO of New York Private Bank & Trust and its operating bank, Emigrant Bank, the country's largest family-run private bank.

On the company's website, Dad summed up the partnership with Howard best when he said, "If you want to have a successful business, partner with Howard Milstein." Howard said about Dad, "He could do half of what he's doing, and it still would be much more than most people. . . . The essence of the man is that he loves to compete and always demanded the best."[2]

It has been estimated that Dad has earned hundreds of millions in the golf business, more than 95 percent of it outside of his tournament earnings. But to do that, he had to always have partners, and if you are committed to a life working with partners, Dad believes you must begin every relationship by seeing the best in others and giving people your trust. Human nature in most of us makes people earn our trust. But in doing so, you can slow the growth process of what you are attempting to accomplish. The harder it is to gain someone's trust, the more hurdles you add to any relationship. Dad had big dreams of what he wanted to achieve, and I marvel at what he's been able to do.

His dedication and respect for the game have allowed him to achieve many of his dreams. And he instilled that same level of high-performance thinking into Nicklaus Companies. Over the years, Dad set out to explain what should be expected from him and everyone who worked with him. That working list became known as "The Nicklaus Way." It has long been a cornerstone for employees, many of whom have been with Dad for thirty-plus years. The words are so impactful, I wanted to share them here:

The Nicklaus Way

- Employees must aspire to reflect and uphold the high standards of character established by Jack Nicklaus and fostered by the Nicklaus Family.
- Inspired by and consistent with the charitable legacy created by our company founders—Jack and Barbara Nicklaus—we will create our own legacy together. Thus, we believe our success must be shared, celebrated and re-invested in the youth of our world and by the communities we serve. This stewardship should be manifested with each service and product we offer.
- Our passion and vision for our company will lead us to superior customer service, will create opportunities for our employees, and separate us from our competitors.
- We will earn the trust of our employees and customers by conducting our business with the highest ethics, values and morals. Our success will be achieved without sacrificing integrity.
- The genuine caring, respect and loyalty for each individual will inspire achievement and excellence in all we do.
- We are responsible for and committed to the success of our customers, clients and partners. In this endeavor, our efforts are unconditional and unwavering.

Dad's business empire hasn't come without struggles, however. The 2008 global financial downturn hit the golf industry hard, and Dad wasn't immune to it. He ran into trouble when the company couldn't meet completion guarantees on two courses (St. Andrews in New York and Bear Creek in California). Both projects cost Dad a lot of money. Dad also suffered financially when he took a portion of the business (not the course-design branch) public in 1996 as Golden Bear Golf. The initial public offering went well, but the stock lost two-thirds of its value over a two-year period.

In a *Golf Digest* interview with Bob Verdi in 2000, Dad explained in retrospect that much of that money lost was because he was so quick to trust other people. And he felt terrible because others who had invested also lost money. When asked if he trusted too many people, Dad said, "Always have."[3]

Dad never wavered. He stayed true to his core values. No matter the setbacks he encountered, Dad has been blessed in his many relationships. Even though he has been burned more than a few times, he continues to see the best in others.

Now in his eighties, Dad has learned how to use other platforms to call out behaviors or performances he admires. Always wanting to bring out the best in others, he has turned into the cool grandfather who has embraced social media and uses it to encourage people to do more. Unlike many celebrities, Dad's postings are more often in praise of others than an acknowledgment of himself. He also posts inspirational messages to encourage others to do well.

Dad remains connected with fans, the golfing community, and the public through his social media accounts and platforms. He has hundreds of thousands of followers across Facebook

(294,000), Twitter (456,000), and Instagram (408,000). He diligently follows the PGA Tour golfers and gives shout-outs to strong performances.

Though reserved on the course during his playing career (most of which occurred when television broadcasts were in black and white), Dad now shows off his outgoing side on the World Wide Web. When Dad posted videos of himself in 2019 making a putt from well off the green in one event and hitting a shot to win another, his followers celebrated him. His playing partner in the second event was entertainer Kid Rock (real name, Bob Ritchie). And as a result of the friendship they developed, Dad has made it a regular habit not only to follow Kid Rock on social media but also to praise him for good things he has done and is doing.

Who says you can't teach on old Bear new tricks?

Dad also uses his newfound platform to raise awareness for causes. In March 2020, after he announced he and Mom had tested positive for COVID-19, Dad posted a short video message on social media that served as a public service announcement as he urged people to "be smart, be safe" when it came to their decisions regarding the coronavirus pandemic.

Another platform that allows Dad to stay in touch with people is YouTube. His tutorials from back in the day can be viewed there. They are still fun to watch and provide a glimpse into his technical skills and success.

John Wesley, who with his brother Charles founded the Methodist movement in the Church of England, once said something to the effect of, "Do all the good you can, in all the ways you can, to all the souls you can, in every place you can, at all the times you can, with all the zeal you can, every time you can."[4]

Whenever I read those words, I think of Mom and Dad. At the beginning of this chapter, I mentioned how they sometimes differed when it came to seeing people in business relationships. But when it comes to charity, their vision is completely aligned. They see the best in others so much that they want to do whatever it takes to help people achieve. I don't ever see them do anything but good. They help people, and they do it all the time.

Part of my struggle is that I feel there are plenty of times people are trying to take advantage of Dad. When I sense that, I want to jump in, especially if his private time and family time are violated. For instance, it seems every time he goes to watch the grandkids at a sporting event a line of professional autograph seekers forms. If I am with him, I sometimes quietly try to stop it.

But Dad is so gracious. He'll wave me off and say with a kind smile, "It's okay, Jackie." Dad gets it. He seems always to take the higher road. His name, his legacy—it's more important for him to be kind than to worry about someone making money from his name.

As I've gone through the process of writing this, it is clear: always seeing the good in others is a Nicklaus trait that I do try to follow.

It is so easy to get down on other people these days. We live in a negative world, where civility and kindness get drowned out in the toxic parts of our culture and social media. I wonder how different things would be if more of us gave each other the benefit of the doubt and showed more grace and forgiveness when people messed up. If we truly want to love each other as we love ourselves, we need to start by seeing the best in other people.

CHAPTER 7

Protect Your Name

It's important to value and respect your name. You carry it forever, right? Dad has always understood the importance of his name. He knew the one thing that would travel with him throughout his life was his name. It was an extension of his family and, regardless of good and bad times, celebrations or burdens, he wanted it to represent quality and help shape our identity when he handed it off to us. Sometimes people try to live up to their names; others try to run away from them.

I learned at an early age the impact my name carried.

I was ten or eleven when I played in a junior golf tournament at Disney World in Orlando. My parents had a Pontiac station wagon for years when I was younger. I will never forget it. But on this trip I caught a ride with my buddy's family to the tournament from Palm Beach to Orlando in their Rolls Royce (that was fun). It was a two-day tourney, and on the second day when we arrived at the course, a local reporter asked to interview me. I was fine with it, but I didn't have time to talk that very second. I was literally running to the 1st tee and asked him if we could talk after the round. The reporter was fine with it, and we agreed to meet after the round.

When it ended, however, my buddy's family wanted to immediately leave and return to the hotel. I explained that I promised to talk to a local reporter, but they said, "No, we need to leave now. Let's go." I couldn't talk them into waiting a few minutes. As I jumped in the back seat of the Rolls Royce, I looked over my shoulder through the back window. I saw the reporter standing with his arms folded, watching us pull away, and shaking his head back and forth. I was sure he thought I was a brat. I felt horrible and mostly was embarrassed. The editor knew my dad and mom and telephoned them that night. He explained the reporter's article was "really rough" on me. The editor also felt it didn't accurately represent our family or me and decided not to publish the story. Mom, however, was mad at me. She explained that, regardless of the circumstances, I'd always have to work 150 percent harder than others because there would always be people who would dismiss or scrutinize what I did because of my name. She said the name of the family I drove with would never end up in headlines. But mine would.

That's true for a lot of kids whose fathers or mothers are successful. Carrying your name in life isn't always easy. I don't think it's isolated to a Jack Nicklaus or a Michael Jordan. It might be true for anyone whose parents are respected in their communities. We don't always think much about it, but older siblings can establish a good name at school, which can be a blessing for their younger brothers or sisters. But the burden of a good name can weigh heavily, and there have been times—especially when I played golf competitively—that my name and its responsibilities weighed on me. The expectations were so high that there was no way I'd ever be able to reach them or match Dad's success on the golf course. It wasn't going to happen.

Integrity has been a core value of Dad's life. He has often explained that golf taught him many valuable lessons and shaped how he has lived. His messages always include integrity, which he believes is understanding who you are and what is right. Here are a few of Dad's favorite quotes on integrity:

Image is what people think we are.
Integrity is what we really are.
—John C. Maxwell[1]

It is true that integrity alone won't make you a leader, but without integrity you will never be one.
—Zig Ziglar[2]

Live so that when your children think of fairness, caring, and integrity, they think of you.
—H. Jackson Brown Jr.[3]

Dad pointed out that people can make whatever they want out of those quotes, but he believes they all say the same thing: you must be true to yourself in whatever you do. That way you can live your life and not have any second thoughts.

He also cites examples on the golf course where a player's integrity can come into play. If your ball lands in a hole in the rough, what do you do? Foot wedge it out when nobody is looking? What if your ball lands behind a tree? What do you do? Pick the ball up and move it so you have a clear shot to the green? Or do you play the shots as they lie?

Dad always reminds fans that golfers must officiate themselves. Golf isn't the NBA, which has a crew chief and two referees on the court. Or professional baseball, which has four umpires on the field. Dad believes when you walk off the course after your round—whether you are a professional golfer who shot 65 or a recreational golfer who shot 95—you should feel good about your round because you followed the rules and played the round correctly. "To me, that's important," Dad says.

There is one time in Dad's career when his actions bothered him. It was the 1974 Open Championship at Royal Lytham and St. Annes Golf Club in Lancashire, England. (Dad finished in third place, five strokes behind winner Gary Player.) It was the 15th hole, and Dad's shot landed in a deep fairway bunker, forty yards from the green. Dad hit his shot, and sand exploded everywhere. He didn't realize it at the time, but the ball went up in the air and landed back in the bunker. Dad had no idea what happened or if the golf ball somehow struck him.

Dad summoned Joseph Dey, who served as executive director of the United States Golf Association from 1934 to 1968 and also served as Commissioner of the PGA Tour from 1969 to 1974. Dad asked Mr. Dey if the ball had struck him. Joe said, "I don't believe it did." To this day, Dad says he's not 100 percent sure the ball didn't hit him (current rules state there is no penalty if the ball hits the player, other players, caddies, or equipment).

As we worked on this book in 2020, it amazes me that is the one time Dad can say he questions whether the correct decision was made. And that was forty-six years ago.

In a 2017 article in *Golf Digest,* Dad talked about the importance of correctly marking your golf ball on the green and player integrity. In the article he shared the story of one of those players who he saw mark his ball incorrectly multiple times and chose to quietly mention it to the tournament rules official. "I mean, it could be accidental," Dad said. "But if it's blatant, then I think it's not fair to the rest of the field to not bring it up."[4]

Golf is known for its infractions, penalties, and thick rulebook. While bending the rules still happens in golf and other sports, Dad believes golfers try very hard to abide by the sport's strict, sacred code: "I think everybody in the game of golf tries to do it the right way, the best way," Dad told *Golf Digest.* "I think there are very, very few people who take advantage of the rules in the game and if somebody does take advantage of the rules of the game, move on and make a lesson of it. I think that's the way we should handle it."[5]

That's what integrity means to Dad. It isn't holding just yourself accountable but the entire game. Just as important, doing the right thing—on the course or off—ensures you are protecting your name and reputation.

Gary Player is one of my all-time favorite people, and he always took steps to protect his name—which leads to one of my all-time favorite stories. When speaking of Gary Player and what a name represents, he is the best. I still call him Uncle Gary. In 1971, when I was eleven years old, the World Cup of Golf was held in Palm Beach Gardens. It is a tournament contested by teams of two representing their respective countries. Dad was teamed with Lee Trevino and represented the United States;

Gary was teamed with Harold Henning and represented South Africa. (Dad and Lee beat Gary and Harold.)

Gary won 167 professional tournaments in fifteen countries, including nine major championships on the PGA Tour. Gary, who was born in 1935, has always been noted for his healthy diet.

When Gary stayed at our home during the tournament, he tried to get me on a health kick. He made me eat plain oatmeal every morning, with no sugar and no milk. It was awful. He wanted me to take cold showers at night and cold baths in the morning. It was miserable. I think I lasted only a few days before I tapped out. When I asked Mom about Uncle Gary's strict health regimen, she smiled, laughed, and said, "Follow me." In the kitchen, he had hidden bags of Snickers and Three Musketeers in the corners of the cabinets—and asked Mom not to tell me about them! Sometimes the steps we take to protect our name can be a little much—though I still laugh over that story and think of Gary every time I have a candy bar.

I was reminded several times in my professional career that while working to protect our family name, I had to be aware of those surrounding me. In golf, no one is closer to you than your caddie—who even wears your name across his back.

Early in my career I couldn't afford to pay a caddie to accompany me overseas, so I either selected or was assigned a caddie at each tournament. Sometimes that doesn't work out well.

In the late 1980s at the Benson and Hedges International Open—it was part of the European Tour's annual schedule from 1972 until the tourney ended in 2003—I carried my own bag for the first practice round on Monday and was assigned a caddie by the tournament for the second round on Tuesday. Unfortunately this guy reeked of alcohol. I thought about making a change, but I decided to remain committed to the process. In Thursday's opening round, my caddie showed up when I was on the 1st tee—hungover from the previous night. In Friday's second round, he showed up after I played ten holes and a spectator from the gallery had been carrying my bag.

I told the caddie I didn't need him and kept the spectator on my bag for the rest of the round. After the round, the caddie wanted to be paid. The minimum caddie payment on the European Tour at that time was $350 (prior to making the cut). Typically, a $150 tip was also included, raising the amount to $500. I gave the caddie $350 and told him goodbye.

Well, the caddie complained to tournament director Ken Schofield that I had shorted him money. Ken suggested that I pay the additional $150 just to be done with the guy and move on. Initially, I declined because I was so upset, and I felt the guy didn't deserve any additional money. When I talked to Dad about it later that evening, he agreed with Ken and suggested I pay. Dad explained that whether the guy's behavior was right or not, I couldn't change it. And, like it or not, this guy probably would have bad-mouthed me to others. Dad felt it wasn't worth the worry. His advice was to just pay the guy so I didn't have to look over my shoulder.

Dad is a longtime believer in and trustee of the First Tee, which began in 1997 as a partnership among the LPGA, the

Masters Tournament, the PGA of America, the PGA Tour, and the USGA to make golf affordable and accessible for all kids. The organization notes it is committed "to helping kids build character strengths and important life skills through the game of golf and providing all kids with access to opportunities for personal growth in a fun and safe environment."[6] The First Tee also teaches kids about the importance of building a reputation for doing the right thing and having integrity.

Dad has spoken multiple times in front of Congress on the importance of First Tee. In a 2014 appearance, he said,

> When I first picked up a club at age 10, it was because I was able to spend time on a golf course with my father. It was there where he and the game helped shape me to be the person I am today. It taught me discipline, integrity, honor and sportsmanship. The first time I threw a club, my father taught me most of those values in one painful lesson.
>
> Golf and the First Tee provide young people role models at a time in their lives when role models are so critical.
>
> What I learned on the golf course many years ago is still important today and those same life lessons are the focus of the First Tee—how to set goals, how to overcome obstacles, how to respect the environment, respect my playing partners and to respect myself.[7]

Dad has always respected himself because he understands what his name represents. He understands the importance of long-term relationships with people and organizations. In actions and words, Dad has shown how a competitor—and a man—should act. He was, and is, a role model to many, including me.

Dad has always wanted to win, saying that's what golf is about. But it's also Dad's integrity that people have admired as much as his ability to win. Dad has said, "If one doesn't have integrity, what else has he got? You have to have integrity in life and be able to make sure that what you do is looked upon as doing the right thing at the right time."

Mom found a lengthy quote that we all believe best describes Dad, all of his wonderful qualities, and what the Nicklaus name represents. We don't know where the quote is from, but it is titled "Inheritance." One year for Christmas I framed a copy for each of my children, who all still have it hanging on their walls.

Inheritance

Not every father is able to leave his children a big estate made up of lands, mortgages and bonds, but any father can bequeath to his children an estate worth infinitely more—one for which they will rise up to call his name blessed.

He can leave an honorable name, a good reputation, the memory of a Godly life and a record of fair dealing. He can teach his children to have a profound respect for a fact, a deep reverence for character, a thirst for knowledge and a willingness to work.

If any youth has all this, they will not need any money that may be willed to them; if they do not have this, no money left them will do them much good.

Charlie—my grandfather, who passed away from pancreatic cancer in 1970 at age fifty-six—was a driving force in my dad's life. Dad thinks of his father every day and continues to honor him in everything he does. Dad credits Grandpa for teaching him how to treat and respect people, how to be a good sport, and how to shake a person's hand and look them in the eye, that your word is your bond, and that you play the hand you are dealt without complaint.

Obviously I knew Grandpa only after Dad was older, and they were best friends. Inseparable. Family always came first to my grandfather, and he passed that conviction on to Dad. To this day, before any decision or business deal Dad makes, he asks himself how it will affect the Nicklaus name. Not his name but the name entrusted to him by his parents. I now do the same.

Building and protecting our names by doing the right thing takes time, but our reputations can be lost quickly. That's something Dad taught me over the years. This lesson is even more important today, with so much attention paid to social media. Times and technology continue to change, but we need to stress to our children how important it is to protect their names.

CHAPTER 8

Be a Parent to Your Children First—and a Best Friend Later

How do you define a best friend?

As a child, your best friend was the person whom you knew was always available when it was time to play. When you were a teen, the person who always had your back became your best friend. But when you grow into adulthood, the definition changes a bit.

From childhood I knew my father always had my best interests at heart, even when I didn't agree with him. When I hit my midtwenties and was about to get married, the question really came to me because I had to choose a best man. It was then, for the first time, I fully realized that my father was my best friend.

That moment really affected me because Dad described his father as his best friend. I believe all of it comes from the way each father chose to raise his children. He was firm but always consistent. He was stern but always caring. And, as a result, each generation of us Nicklauses has realized no friend cared more for us than our fathers.

Charlie and Helen Nicklaus married in 1937 and had two children—Dad, born in 1940, and Marilyn, born in 1943. Grandpa was a pharmacist and lived in an apartment above his drugstore in Columbus near The Ohio State University campus. Grandpa had attended Ohio State and was a natural athlete. He played various sports growing up, including football, basketball, and baseball, and later played semi-pro football. As a youth, Charlie was a scratch golfer and a city champion in tennis. He also saw Bobby Jones win the 1926 U.S. Open at Scioto Country Club. Our family later had a golf membership there, and Dad developed his golf game on that course. (Dad's love for Bobby Jones was also passed down by his father.)

As he grew older, Grandpa's interest in golf waned, but then when he was in his midthirties, he injured his ankle playing volleyball. The ankle never healed properly, and his physician encouraged him to begin playing golf again since it allowed him to walk without further damaging his ankle. Grandpa joined the Scioto Country Club, where Dad caddied for him, and picked up golf for the first time during the course's summer program.

Like his father, Dad was a natural athlete and played multiple sports before he decided on golf. Like most kids, Dad could be rambunctious. One story that still cracks me up took place when Dad was about ten years old. He was dressed in a full football uniform—helmet, shoulder pads, and pants—at his home. As the babysitter walked upstairs from the basement with a laundry basket full of clothes, Dad was set in a three-point football stance at the top of the stairs. He said, "One, two, three, four, five, six, seven, eight, nine, ten. Hut! Hut!" He tackled the babysitter as she reached the top step, and both went rolling down into the basement. Thankfully, nobody was hurt. When my grandma returned home, the babysitter announced as she departed, "I will not be back."

In high school Dad played quarterback on the football team, was a catcher on the baseball team, and was an honorable mention All-Ohio selection in basketball as a shooting guard for the Upper Arlington Golden Bears. He was also recruited by college basketball programs, including Ohio State.

Dad described his decision to pursue golf as a "process of elimination." Dad's hands weren't big enough to properly grip a football when Ohio's weather turned damp and cold. Baseball didn't work out for him because it coincided with the golf season. And at five-foot-ten, Dad felt he wasn't tall enough or quick enough to play basketball at an elite program like Ohio State.

On the golf course Dad was coached at Scioto by club pro Jack Grout. Jack previously played on the PGA Tour and was Dad's instructor throughout his amateur and professional careers. Dad proved to be a quick learner. After only a few weeks of lessons, Mr. Grout often called Dad out to show the other kids how to hit a fade or a draw or how to take a proper divot. My dad loved to practice and was at the golf course so often that it actually caused a financial challenge for his father.

In an article that Dad wrote for the Players' Tribune and titled "Letter to My Younger Self," he described his memories of that time and its impact on his life:

> Then one day, there's going to be a bill in the mail. Dad will go grab it. Then he'll yell your name in that voice . . . that voice is trouble, you know it. He'll be holding a bill from Scioto.

"Three hundred dollars, Jack?"

At this moment, hold your ground, young man.

You'll say this to him. "Dad, you told me you wanted me to learn how to play golf. . . ."

He'll say, "Yes, but $300 worth of range balls?"

Now you got him.

"I don't just want to learn the game—I want to be great at it."[1]

Grandpa was a close friend of Ohio State football coach Woody Hayes, who lived a few blocks from Grandpa's pharmacy. When Woody was in the pharmacy one day, Grandpa, who'd played professional football, said to him, "Jack's thinking of giving up football—and it's killing me."

Woody quickly replied, "Charlie, I know about your son's golf talents. You keep him as far away from my sport as you can."

Hayes, who coached at Ohio State for twenty-eight seasons (1951 to 1978) and won five national titles, followed Dad at the amateur and professional levels early in his career. A story shared by PGATour.com was an example of Coach Hayes's inner fire and loyalty:

> Jack was emerging as a rival to the popular Arnold Palmer, and the gallery treated him rudely—especially at the 1962 U.S. Open in Palmer's backyard at Oakmont. Hayes, so incensed by the crowd's reaction, had to be restrained from going after one fan. The guy who restrained him was Charlie Nicklaus.
>
> "If Woody liked you and supported you, you'd better not

be saying something against who he's supporting," Jack said. "That was Woody. He was something else."[2]

•

Coach Hayes, who passed away in 1987, always loved the relationship my grandpa and Dad shared. I remember Coach Hayes visited Grandpa on Christmas Day 1969, when he was sick. We had traveled to Ohio from Florida to spend the holidays with Grandpa and Grandma. That Christmas Day was the last day Grandpa was well enough to eat a meal with his family. Coach Hayes and Grandpa spent hours together and talked about family and life. I know the bond between the two was special and was one that impacted Dad too.

I was eight years old when Grandpa died on February 19, 1970. A few months earlier, in the fall of 1969, Dad and Grandpa attended an Ohio State football game, and Dad noticed his father's skin had a jaundiced color to it. Grandpa was diagnosed with pancreatic cancer around Thanksgiving, and his quick death was so sad and very tough on everyone.

I was scared at the funeral, not knowing what to do, being so young. Mom asked me to stand next to Dad to offer him support. As I looked up at Dad, who was standing near Grandpa's casket, I saw tears in his eyes. That was hard. It was the first time I ever saw Dad cry. It took me years to talk to him about it, and when I did, what he said surprised me. His first words were "Jackie, my dad lived for me and my success."

Dad wasn't just sad that his father, his best friend, had died. He was sad because, in his mind, he hadn't played golf that was good enough to make his father proud. Dad felt that in the two years prior, he had not worked as hard as he could have on his golf game and had let his dad down.

Grandpa was at Dad's side during tournaments, from the youth circuit to the professional tour, and was his biggest fan. When Dad was young, he once complained to his father that he made him nervous on the golf course. Grandpa told Dad he'd better get used to it—he planned to be at every event.

Grandpa couldn't have been happier or prouder when Dad turned professional in late 1961 and enjoyed immediate success. That success, however, dipped (by Dad's standards) in 1968 and 1969. He won five tournaments in forty-five starts, and for the first time since his rookie season, he failed to rank among the top three on the PGA Tour money list. It was also the first time since 1964 he did not win a major.

That victory drought in the majors, combined with Grandpa's death, proved to be a significant window in Dad's career. Grandpa knew that Dad felt bad about it, and in the last words the two spoke to each other, Grandpa told Dad, "Don't think it ain't been sweet."

Dad, though, had a sense of guilt, believing he could have made it sweeter if he had been more committed on the course in those last two years of Grandpa's life. Dad has always believed we need to give 110 percent and try our best in anything we attempt. We are here for only a short period, and it's important to make the most of our time.

Grandpa's death forced Dad to refocus on playing. After his father passed, Dad thought, *You know what? I'm going to get back to work. I'm going to make my father proud.*

For the first time, Dad also admitted in the late '60s that he was probably overweight and out of shape. While he is known as the Golden Bear, his initial nickname on the PGA Tour wasn't as flattering. He was called "Fat Jack" by fans and the media for his husky frame. While some of the other golfers wore tailor-made trousers and T-shirts, which provided plenty of movement, Dad's clothes were either too tight or too big. He had a crew cut and chubby cheeks. Though Dad was always concerned about what a physical transformation might do to his game, the 1969 Ryder Cup was the first time he said he got physically tired while playing golf. When he returned to Florida, he told Mom he intended to lose twenty pounds from his 210-pound frame.

Dad's strategy was twofold. He followed a few diet plans and jogged on the golf course between shots while he played and practiced. Dad lost twenty pounds during the first month and eventually got down to 185 pounds, where he stayed for the remainder of his career. The transformation was impressive. He grew out his blond hair, his clothes fit perfectly, and he had those steely blue eyes. Some say he looked like a male model. His golf game continued to turn heads too. He went six years—105 tournaments—without missing a cut.

Five months after Grandpa died, Dad had regrouped, winning his second of three Open Championships—which he dedicated to his dad—in an 18-hole Sunday playoff over Doug Sanders at the Old Course in St. Andrews, Scotland. From 1970 to 1973, Dad won twenty-two tournaments, including five majors, and was the PGA Tour's top money winner three consecutive years (1971, 1972, and 1973).

Grandpa is not with Dad physically, but even now he's with Dad spiritually every day.

Without hesitation I can say Dad is my best friend. It's not like we are around each other all the time, but I know he's there when I need him. You want your best friend to affirm and recognize your decisions and accomplishments, and I look for that from Dad. I still want and need his approval. Even at my age, his approval still provides a sense of well-being and self-confidence.

And what's very cool is that in recent years, I have heard a couple of my kids say I am their best friend. I think that's a unique gift that has been passed down from my grandfather to Dad to me and now to my kids. It's not healthy to be best friends with your children when they are little, especially since what they need is more discipline and guidance. But if you love and support them, they just might call you their best friend when they reach adulthood.

CHAPTER 9

Stay Laser-Focused on What You Can Control

After I committed myself to pursuing a career in golf, Dad worked to help me improve my game. He worked with me on how to become a better putter, to be better around the green with my short game, and to be prepared and act like a champion. What he couldn't help me with was my greatest challenge because he didn't understand. Dad just went out and did it! Pressure and anxiety weren't part of his makeup on the golf course. But they were part of mine. Golf is an individual sport. Golfers are responsible for what happens to them during a tournament.

When I graduated from the University of North Carolina and turned professional, I started sessions with Dr. Bob Rotella. Bob was the well-known director of sports psychology at the University of Virginia for twenty years. He focused on the mental aspects of golf, and his lengthy client list included Hall of Fame golfers, such as Tom Kite and Nick Price, in addition to more modern stars, such as Rory McIlroy and Padraig Harrington.

Bob once gave me a homework assignment, and it might seem

odd, but it was ten questions to ask Dad. One of the questions I specifically recall was how Dad concentrated on the course when there was so much going on around him. In fact, most of the questions focused on concentration and how Dad consistently performed at such a high level over the course of his career. Dad's concentration showed in his performances at the elite level. For instance, Dad holds the record for most under-par rounds in the PGA Championship (fifty-three) and the record for the most rounds in the '60s in the PGA Championship (forty-one). He also played in the most consecutive majors (156), stretching from the 1957 U.S. Open to the 1998 U.S. Open.

I asked Dad the questions, but he never answered them. Dad is rather old-school and was reluctant to embrace the benefits of working with a sports psychologist. He wasn't convinced that Bob could help me. "If I have to concentrate, I just do it," Dad said. "If I need to shout, I just do it."

"Dad, you aren't really helping me!" I said.

To which he shrugged and said, "That's the best answer I can give you."

What I learned in that moment is that, like many elite athletes, Dad couldn't explain to me what he did that made him special. We all know how few greats actually become great coaches because often what they do and how they think aren't transferable knowledge. What I proved was that it wasn't transferable genetically. That was the last time I tried to get Dad to help me with Bob's homework questions.

Golf has always been considered the thinking man's game. There's much more to golf than striking the ball. Dad's concentration routine enabled him to fixate on his shots and what he wanted to accomplish. Dad's focus on the task at hand is legendary and is credited as a major part of his success, especially in the majors, where he became very difficult to beat. At the majors, Dad led outright or shared the lead after three rounds twelve times in his career and went on to win ten of those tournaments.

While Dad wouldn't help me with the homework questions, the exercise led to several impactful conversations, conversations that went far beyond golf. He shared with me that I would be better at anything and everything I would do in life if I would stay locked in on the moment, not worrying about what happened previously or what would happen next. It is almost cliché to say you have to focus only on the things you can control. But I didn't have to hear Dad say the cliché—I could watch him live it out. This is a lesson he's worked for forty years to teach me.

And one I will work for the next forty years to teach my children.

One example of Dad's focus that I had the chance to witness occurred on the 4th green in the Masters at Augusta National. I caddied for Dad, and he had a four- to five-foot putt, left to right, for a par. At this time the hole had a hedge of very thick and tall bamboo trees surrounding the green. And beyond the trees was a city road. The traffic light at the four-way stop was literally twenty-five to thirty yards from where Dad stood on the green.

As Dad stood over his putt, the golf gallery was quiet. I stood on the edge of the green when Dad started to pull the putter head back. At that moment the sound of screeching tires, a hard skid that lasted a few seconds, followed by a loud crash filled the air. Everyone in the gallery was startled. I looked up and out toward the street. I looked back at Dad, and he never lifted his head. He continued with his putt—and made it. He bent over, picked his golf ball out of the cup, and handed it to me along with his putter.

I asked him, "Dad, did you not hear that?"

He looked at me and said, "Hear what? What are you talking about?"

"There was a car accident, right there," I said, pointing to the intersection.

Dad said, "I didn't hear a thing."

I don't know how he did it. But when he was dialed in, nothing interrupted his concentration. He stayed in the present. He didn't think about the next shot or how he got there; he was dialed in on that shot.

Charlie Mechem, the former LPGA Commissioner, is one of Dad's dearest and "longest tenured" friends. Charlie also experienced Dad's intense focus when they met to discuss a business relationship in 1970. At the time, Charlie was the chairman and CEO of Taft Broadcasting Company. TBC wanted Dad to design two public golf courses in Cincinnati across from Kings Island amusement park, another one of its properties under construction at the time. Charlie met Dad in Jacksonville, Florida, where he was in a tournament, to discuss the specifics. Dad agreed to build an 18-hole public course and an 18-hole executive course, and the deal was signed.

The following day Charlie attended the tournament and followed Dad. As Charlie shared in a story he authored for Golf.com—"6 Life Lessons Jack Nicklaus Taught Me That Everyone Can Learn From"—he witnessed Dad's incredible focus. Charlie had positioned himself between a green and a tee box to make sure Dad saw him. As Dad walked off the green and to that tee box, Charlie wrote that Dad "looked me straight in the eye and walked on without a word or a gesture. I was shocked!"

Charlie relayed the story with one of Dad's business colleagues a few minutes later. Charlie thought he might have unknowingly offended or insulted Dad during their business meeting the night before. Dad's colleague laughed and said, "Charlie, Jack never even saw you. His concentration is such that he sees nothing except the next hole in his mind's eye." Charlie shared: "That's when I first experienced the power of Jack's incredible concentration, which paid dividends over and over again through his career."[1]

Heck, at another tournament Dad didn't even notice Chicago Bears football coach Mike Ditka waving and standing near him during a practice round. I was caddying for Dad and saw Coach Ditka in the crowd to our left near the tee box. Coach smiled and waved at us, but Dad didn't react. He hit his tee shot and we marched off. Knowing that Dad was a big fan of football and Coach Ditka, I said, "Dad, that was Mike Ditka!" Dad snapped out of his fog and said, "What? Where? I love Mike." I turned and pointed out Coach Ditka, and Dad made a beeline to him to say hello.

I have spent my life around some of the most high-performing people in the world, and I've never seen anyone manage his or her mind like Dad. No wonder he was no help with my homework.

The ability to compartmentalize and focus are important skills to have in helping achieve success. You see it in those who are the very best at what they do. They can take what's happening elsewhere and set it aside for the moment, focus on what's required, and not be as affected as the rest of the world is. How many times, for example, have you heard about an athlete who may have lost a family member and the next night scored sixty points in a basketball game? Gosh, how does that happen?

Dad had one of those stories too.

On the eve of the 1981 Open Championship at the Royal St. George's Golf Club in Sandwich, England, Dad took a phone call that nearly derailed his ability to play golf. Back in the States, my brother Steve had dropped off his date and was on his way home when he fell asleep on the Jack Nicklaus Freeway in Columbus. His car crossed the median, flipped six times, and ended up on the opposite side of the highway. Steve was fine, thankfully. He got out of the car and somehow walked home. Dad was obviously extremely upset when he received the news.

When he realized Steve was safe, he decided to stay and play. But in that first round, Dad shot an 83. Incredibly, relieved that Steve was okay, he pulled himself together emotionally and shot a 66 in the second round to make the tournament's cut. Dad finished tied for 23rd, quite a golf accomplishment given the circumstances.

When Dad was on the PGA Tour, he had family, he had golf, and he had business. Whichever one needed his attention in any moment, he was fully dedicated and locked in. I think that ability to compartmentalize kept him fresh for the other two.

All of us have a lot going on in our lives, from work to our children to projects at home. There are plenty of days when it seems too much. But Dad was always able to focus on whatever he could control. Despite whatever was going on in the other parts of life, he was able to focus on the matter at hand. Giving whatever was in front of him his full attention, Dad was able to excel on the course, in business, and when it came to raising a family. There's a lesson for all of us here, to focus on what we can actually control instead of worrying over things we can't.

CHAPTER 10

Give More Than You Take in Your Relationships

Many believe marriage is a 50-50 proposition. My parents, who will celebrate their sixty-first wedding anniversary in July 2021, have calculated their own equation for a long marriage.

Mom and Dad believe a successful relationship is 95 percent give to 5 percent take, both ways. That may not sound possible, but they have proven otherwise. Two key elements are required to make this work. The first is that neither party can keep a scorecard of places where they've given to the other for purposes of comparison. The second is that both have to be committed to the 95 percent give to 5 percent take model. This can also sound quite complicated.

How could both of them give 95 percent?

It took writing this book for me to realize that my parents began every discussion about family plans with each of them thinking first of the other. And by doing that, they found a relationship rubric that didn't just allow both of them to live fulfilled lives, it also allowed them to raise five pretty successful children. As I have sat down with my parents to discuss their success, they've shared how the model has changed over time. But it always began with empathy for the other before their individual needs.

Even though Dad knew his craft as a professional golfer would keep him on the road often, his greatest responsibility was to return home as fast as possible. He vowed never to be away from home longer than two weeks at a time. (I know that might sound crazy to some, but in his profession it's not uncommon to be gone many weeks at a time.) Other than a seventeen-day trip to South Africa for a series of exhibitions with Gary Player, I don't think Dad ever missed that mark when I was young. That's amazing.

Through the entirety of his marvelous achievements, despite the phone calls from presidents, visits with kings, and adulation from crowds, Dad made being a husband the most important part of life. Being a dad was second. When Dad returned home, he didn't talk golf. His focus was on us. Dad saw golfers on the PGA Tour who had no family life outside of golf and often wondered how they did it.

By being so in sync and living lives in service of each other, Mom and Dad weren't just a great team. They were incredible role models for us, the five kids. Now they are relationship role models to twenty-two grandchildren and even many friends in the community.

Dad is always quick to credit Mom for all her support, but he's barely through any sentence about her without Mom interjecting how grateful she was for the hard work he did to provide for us.

Dad was the disciplinarian when he was home, but Mom managed the children and the household while he traveled the globe to play golf. Don't think for a second Mom didn't discipline us when Dad was gone.

There were words I uttered as a kid that today wouldn't raise an eyebrow. They might be words kids hear or see on the internet or television every hour of the day. If I said God's name in vain, Mom marched me into the bathroom, where I had to take a bite from the bar of Dial soap. Call me a slow learner, but Mom washed my mouth out with soap several times. And if you haven't had the experience, it tasted awful! If we did something wrong, Mom immediately took care of it. She did not, as I am told some mothers do, wait until our father came home to lay down the law. I would later learn Mom did this intentionally because she didn't want the first conversation when Dad came through the door to involve what he had to do to straighten us out.

Mom believed Dad needed to come home to a happy family to be successful. This entire conversation might sound completely old-fashioned to some younger couples today, but I can only point them to one number—sixty-one. And that wasn't my dad's lowest score on the golf course.

As Dad has gotten older, the percentage pendulum has swung. Today Dad makes many life adjustments to fully support Mom's many endeavors. Dad laughed when he said he was lucky to get by the first fifty years in their marriage.

"The first fifty years are the hardest," he joked.

Humor is another important component to their marriage.

Nobody would guess in a million years what an incredible prankster my mom is. She is known to sneak rubber insects (roaches and ants, specifically) into our meals, most often in restaurants.Mom got family friend Van Lefferdink good during a trip to New Zealand. Mom, Dad, and Van were at the table for breakfast, when Van found a rubber roach peeking out of his oatmeal. On another occasion Mom nearly scared me to death when she hid a rubber snake in my luggage at a tournament in Baltimore.

It was important to both of them that they were able to laugh at themselves and laugh with each other. Yes, Dad still tells some of the worst dad jokes of all time. But while the grandkids might roll their eyes, Mom still laughs at every one. They also both love to look for humor in many stories. If you listen to the two of them reflect on some period of their lives, almost every discussion is rooted in an element of humor. And they truly do finish each other's sentences—or punch lines.

Part of what makes them special is how many of Dad's travel experiences they were able to share together. Of the one hundred majors Dad played in, Mom missed only two—the 1963 Masters when Steve was born four days later and the 1973 Open Championship when Michael was due early. When their last child left for college, Dad instituted a new rule: if Mom didn't go with him to any tournament, he wouldn't go.

Early in their marriage and for a number of years in golf, there weren't many spouses along on the road. Mom was an exception. When the calendar permitted, the family came along. The commitments—Dad's promise to never be gone more than two weeks, Mom's work to hold the household together without complaint, their desire to be together even on the road—allowed them to manage any rough patches. Mom has said when she was young she never heard the word *divorce*. Back then couples worked it out. Today it seems if there's a bump in the road, couples want to take the exit ramp.

Because of Dad's constant travels, Mom was often asked during his playing career what it was like to be a "golf widow." Mom was aghast! She never felt that way because Dad always made her a part of his life.

During one tournament, Mom stopped after the 7th hole to talk to the wife of one of the other golfers. In the car after the round, Dad asked Mom, "Where were you on the 8th hole?"

Mom replied, "There were forty thousand people on the course. How did you know I wasn't there on the 8th hole?"

"You weren't there," Dad said.

"I wasn't there, but how did you know?" Mom asked.

Dad explained he recognized Mom's walk, and he always *knew* where she was on the course.

Mom was stunned. "I never thought he even knew I was on the golf course," she said.

Mom is such a warrior. During the 2000 Memorial Tournament in Columbus, Ohio, Mom motioned for me as she stood near the 14th green and 15th tee box, watching Dad play. She explained she could not move because of excruciating pain in her back and she needed my help. I knew it had to be bad because Mom never wants any attention. In an effort not to alarm anyone, I casually walked out of the corner of Dad's line of sight. When I was beyond Mom's view, I went into a full sprint to the medical staff and explained the situation. They rushed out to Mom, who watched Dad tee off at No. 15. The medical staff wanted to take

Mom off the course, but she politely and sternly refused. She also declined to sit in a golf cart!

Mom missed Dad on the 16th hole, but then walked gingerly up a fifty-foot rise to the 17th green to watch Dad's approach. She could barely walk down the 18th fairway, but she watched Dad putt out and then allowed us to take her to the hospital. There, to the surprise of all, she was diagnosed with a kidney stone.

Some of the stories of their marital adventures almost sound as if they are taken from the script of a black-and-white television show. For example, there's the time Mom took matters into her own hands the evening prior to Nan's birth in 1965.

Dad had played in an exhibition at Scioto Country Club in Columbus, with Bob Hope, James Garner, and the club pro earlier in the day. (Mom, very pregnant with Nan, had followed Dad's round in a golf cart.) Everyone returned to the house for dinner. Dad, Bob Hope, James Garner, and the group were playing pool downstairs when Mom called down to ask Dad if he'd light the charcoal grill.

Dad said, "I'll be up in a minute."

Ten minutes later Mom asked Dad if he was ready to cook the steaks.

"Barbara, the fire's not even ready," Dad said.

Mom, of course, had lit the grill.

A short time later Mom asked everyone if they were ready to eat.

"Barb, I haven't even fixed the steaks!" Dad said.

Mom, of course, had cooked the steaks.

During dinner, Mom excused herself and walked to the bedroom. She didn't return for thirty or so minutes, prompting Dad to go check on her. It was about 10:30 p.m., and Mom was in labor. She said, "Don't worry about it. I've called the doctor. I don't want to interrupt dinner. I will take a taxi."

Dad went into panic mode. He told the guys, "My wife's having a baby. I have to get her to the hospital." Bob Hope, James Garner, and the others were gone in thirty seconds. Nan was born less than two hours later at 12:15 a.m. Because of the company that night, the family story goes that if Nan had been a boy, she would have been named Robert James after Bob Hope and James Garner.

Nan has heard the story so many times, she named her fourth son Robert James!

Dad has often said he was touched by an angel when he met Mom on the campus of Ohio State. She is "the guiding light," he says, "of everything we've tried to accomplish." Dad clearly admits the best decision he ever made was to marry Barbara Bash. Bette Midler's rendition of "The Rose" is so relevant to their relationship. I have watched the decisions Dad has made through his life and have been impacted greatly by his passion and commitment to family, career, gifting, and mentoring. Yet he has always rightly credited Mom with holding down the fort for the family. Mom is truly the wind beneath Dad's wings.

As I've already said, both Mom and Dad were from Columbus and attended rival high schools. They first met during their freshman year at Ohio State in 1957, and they were engaged two years later around Christmas. During the summer between their junior and senior years, on July 23, 1960, they were married. Their wedding day probably made clear to Mom what life was going to be like as Barbara Nicklaus—Dad played thirty-six holes of golf earlier on his wedding day! Even on their honeymoon trip, when in Atlantic City, he included a few stops along the way to play golf.

Dad never cracked under pressure on the golf course, but that wasn't always the case at the hospital's newborn nursery.

When I was born in 1961, Dad—coming off his second U.S. Amateur—was in Cincinnati for a golf tournament. Mom was nine months pregnant with me, but she encouraged Dad to play in the tournament. Before one of his rounds, Mom telephoned Dad from the hospital in Columbus to inform him he was a father. This story has two endings. First, Dad won the tournament. Second, when Dad made it to the hospital, asked the nurse which baby was his, and she pointed me out—he fainted. Dad actually fainted at the birth of *four* of his children! When Michael was born, Dad brought his own smelling salts to the hospital to make sure he remained upright. Mom told PGATour.com that Dad was out for fifteen minutes when Nan was born. "He was in the recovery room longer than I was," Mom teased.[1]

Mom carted me around to a number of tournaments as an infant, but for the 1962 Masters in Augusta, she left me at home with the grandparents. Dad, twenty-two at the time, was making his first professional appearance and fourth overall at the Masters. Early in the tournament, Mom was on the Augusta National patio overlooking the 1st tee with other wives, questioning her decision to travel without me.

One of the wives—Lloyd Mangrum's wife, Eleta—offered Mom pointed advice that she took to heart for the rest of Dad's career. Eleta pointed her finger at Mom and said, "You had Jack long before that baby was born, and you hope to have Jack long after that baby is gone. So you grow up and be a wife." Eleta probably never knew what she did for Mom and Dad's marriage. Mom said she always remembered those words and gave her full attention to Dad when she believed he needed it.

Mom also offered advice when she felt it was appropriate. On one occasion the wife of a top golfer called and asked Mom if she had read an article that had been written about the woman's husband. It wasn't a flattering article, and she said she couldn't wait to show it to her husband to see how he would react. She felt her husband needed to know about the article and knew he'd be "pissed" about it.

Mom asked her, "Why in the world would you ever show that article to him?" Mom explained that if an article like that had been written about Dad, she'd throw it away and hope he never saw it because it would only upset him. Mom sheltered Dad from any form of negativism because it wasn't productive for him. Mom has always said men are simple, and they need three things: food, love, and encouragement—and they will be fine.

Dad and Mom have been such amazing role models. I have always aspired to be like them because of their relationship. Yet I suspect, like any parents, they have endured some pretty tough moments. But I can't tell you exactly when those moments came because they never let their children witness their issues—in fact, I have never heard my parents raise their voices at each other. As I have gotten older, I have been more aware of those hurdles and come to realize the way they handle friction is just different from the rest of us. Mom might go through the silent routine. Or Dad might shut down, too, when they disagree. Dad concedes there are days when he gets up on the wrong side of the bed—and everybody around him soon knows it. He is a perfectionist, very organized, and likes to get everything done as soon as possible. Mom brings patience and a soothing demeanor—both have been good for Dad.

Dad has often asked himself what his life would have been like if he hadn't met Mom. Because of their relationship I grew up thinking that couples got married, held hands, and walked off into the sunset happily ever after. Of course, it's not like that at all in most cases.

There was a time in my life during my first marriage when I looked in the mirror and asked myself if I had given that relationship all I had. My answer was yes. Due to marital struggles at the time, however, my life was a mess. I really believed I was a failure. I sat down with my wife, the mother of my kids, and said, "You know, I am dying inside. We have to get divorced. I can't do this anymore." A few days later I went to my parents' house and told them my decision. Mom was the only one home, and when I told her, she started to cry. Immediately I told Mom, "Don't be sad."

"I am not sad," Mom answered. "I have been waiting for you to tell me this for the last fifteen years. Your father and I knew you were not happy." Mom's tears were more like tears of relief.

Mom and Dad later explained that, as parents, it was difficult to interject their opinions in certain aspects of their kids' lives.

They felt marriage was a line they did not want to cross because, if they did, they could easily lose a son or a daughter.

Mom and Dad's relationship not only impacted me as a son and father, it is one my children truly respect and idolize. My parents have set such an incredible example of how two people should love, care for, and respect one another over the years. They have their own give-and-take equation that works perfectly for them since they both give more than they take. We might think that a marriage, or any important relationship, is a 50-50 proposition, but to make it work, we need to make sure we give a lot more than 50 percent.

CHAPTER 11

Build Your Legacy Every Day

Dad wants to be remembered as someone who gave more than he received. That's the epitome of what it means to build a legacy. Dad knows the importance of passing along life lessons to people, and he wants to live the best life he possibly can.

Naturally, when most people think about Dad's legacy, they connect it to golf.

Dad's idol was Bobby Jones, the most successful amateur golfer ever. When Dad was fifteen, he first met Mr. Jones at the U.S. Amateur at the Country Club of Virginia. Jones, fifty-three years old at the time, had come out to watch Dad. Needless to say, Jones's presence and graciousness made a big impression.

When Dad decided to turn professional in November 1961, he received a letter from Jones. The letter encouraged Dad to remain an amateur but suggested that if he was going to turn pro, Dad should take a close look at Jones's friends at Spalding. We always had a family laugh about that. Dad's decision was easy. He wanted to play against the game's best at the professional level—money and endorsements were never a motivation. Jones held the record for the most major titles, thirteen at the time. Twelve years later Dad won his fourteenth major title to surpass his idol's record.

One of Dad's favorite photographs is a picture of him carrying four-year-old Gary off the 18th green in the second round of the 1973 PGA Championship in Cleveland. I know it made for a cool photo and memory, but Mom wasn't happy Gary had slipped away from her to run onto the green. And as his mother, she was embarrassed. Later she disciplined Gary, who sat quietly and took it. But I have to come clean when I tell this story. I'm the one who encouraged Gary, who is eight years my junior, to run out on the green. Making that memory even better, this was the tournament Dad won, in his home state, for his fourteenth major to surpass Bobby Jones's record.

Dad is often asked if he had one more round of golf to play, who would be in his foursome. His answer surprised me. Dad does not want to play in a foursome for his last round. He wants to play in a fivesome—with his four sons. (The first time Dad did play in a tournament with all four of us was the BMW Charity Pro-Am at the Cliffs in Greenville, South Carolina, in 2003.)

Dad's favorite courses are Pebble Beach, Augusta National, and the Old Course at St. Andrews. He loves the beauty of Pebble Beach and cherishes what it has meant to him and his career. He won the U.S. Open, U.S. Amateur, and several Crosby Events there. Dad's name and Augusta National are synonymous, thanks to his six Masters titles. It also might be the best membership golf course because it can be converted from tournament play to membership play, not an easy task at many elite courses. Dad also loves the Old Course at St. Andrews for its place in history and his two Open Championships there.

Pebble Beach, Augusta, and the Old Course at St. Andrews epitomize the word *legacy*, each combining history with excellence. But the fact that he would play his final round of golf with his sons—no matter where—says everything you really need to know.

When Dad considers his golf legacy, the majors are important, but his real pride comes out at Muirfield Village Golf Club. In 1984 I had the chance to caddie for Dad when he beat Andy Bean, a good friend of our family, on the third sudden-death playoff hole. It was a special moment because it was Dad's first win in two years and his seventieth PGA Tour victory. There was so much drama and excitement over those final holes. Andy made seven birdies over an 11-hole stretch and pulled even with Dad at 9 under par with two holes left.

After Andy drove safely on No. 17—the 71st hole of the tournament—Dad hit the most God-awful drive off the tee. It sailed out of bounds, far right and over a house on the course. The golf ball eventually settled under a picnic table on the pool deck of a residence. It was completely out of character for Dad. I had never seen him hit a golf shot so badly in that type of a situation. I figured he had lost the tournament on that shot.

Even though Dad's next shot split the fairway and his approach settled on the green, around thirty or so feet from the flag, my mind wandered. As I tended the flag for Dad's putt, I still thought of his errant tee shot. Out of the corner of my eye, I noticed Dad motioning to me to pull the pin from the cup. Under the rules at that time, Dad would have been penalized two shots if his putt—about five feet from the cup—hit the pin. I quickly pulled the pin, and Dad's putt rolled in for a bogey 5, counting the out-of-bounds tee shot penalty.

That left Dad one stroke behind Andy and with one hole left to play in regulation. Dad birdied the 18th, and Andy had the chance to win the tourney, but he missed a four-foot birdie putt. The pair each birdied the first extra hole in sudden-death, parred the second, and Dad won the tourney on the third hole (No. 17) when Andy missed his short par putt.

Dad has always said there will be days when you get kicked in the shin, but it's important to never give up. Those words help define Dad's legacy.

Pride is a part of any legacy.

The PGA Tour does not have a policy against chewing tobacco or smoking cigarettes on the course. Like the rest of the population sixty years ago, more golfers smoked than didn't, and Dad was among those who puffed on the course.

But a few months after winning the U.S. Open in 1962, Dad saw himself in a highlights video from the tournament with a cigarette dangling from his lips. In fact, both Dad and Arnold Palmer smoked on the course throughout the tournament. Dad thought it was a poor example for children watching, and that was the last time he ever smoked on the golf course. He eventually quit smoking altogether around 1980.

Still, golfers continued to smoke on the course, and the 1984 Memorial wasn't an exception. My job as Dad's caddie was to help him win the tournament. But Dad also wanted to make sure fans looked favorably at the Muirfield Village Golf Club. He wanted them to think of it as a beautiful, special place, as opposed to thinking it looked like every other golf course. For four straight days during the tournament, as Dad played his round, he had me pick up every cigarette butt he saw on the ground. We walked between the gallery ropes from greens to tees, and whenever he would see a cigarette butt, he'd say, "Pick that up, pick that up, pick that up."

Thankfully, I wore my red painter's pants that were standard fare for me in college at North Carolina. Everyone else hated the pants, distinguished by their many pockets, but I loved them. Mom probably tried to throw them away four different times, but I dug them out of the garbage every time she did. So I wore my red painter's pants and caddie vest, and I literally filled my pockets three to four times a round with cigarette butts that Dad pointed out on the ground. It seemed as though every time I passed a garbage can, I was pulling cigarette butts from every pocket. If I had any inclination of smoking a cigarette before that event, there's no way in the world I would ever smoke a cigarette after. The smell was disgusting.

Looking back, as small a task as it was, I can see picking up the cigarette butts was all about a legacy. Even as Dad tried to win a golf tournament, he wanted to show pride in his home and the course he had created. He also wanted to show that no job—even picking up cigarette butts—was beneath any of us (or at least me).

There are many lessons here—about having pride in your

creation and in your work, about raising children and instilling a work ethic, and about Dad always wanting us to go above and beyond. But the greatest lesson is about the importance of building your legacy every day.

I have given two speeches about Dad over the years that touch on my sense of his legacy.

Sportscaster and family friend Jim Nantz had asked Dad if he could help raise money in his father's name for the fight against Alzheimer's. The fundraiser was played at Monterey Country Club and Cypress Point Club in Pebble Beach, California. Dad said he would be part of the event if he could bring all five of his children.

After the first day of play at Cypress Point, Jim motioned for me to get in the car with him. As we drove along the California coastline, Jim asked if I could speak and present my dad at the charity dinner that evening. Jim wanted the theme to focus on what Dad meant to me, adding that he often thought about his dad, who passed away from Alzheimer's at age seventy-nine in 2008. Jim's relationship with his father inspired his book, *Always by My Side*.

I accepted his invitation and addressed the crowd that night:

> With the exception of the 1960 U.S. Amateur, I have been at Monterey Peninsula for all of Dad's majors: 1972, 1982, and 2000. Dad is golf's greatest champion. He has been, first and foremost, my dad, the finest man I have ever known. Kind, thoughtful, strong, reliable, involved, wise, engaging and loving.

> Fathers make an important difference in the lives of their children. . . . I speak now for my brothers, Michael, Steve, Gary; and my sister, Nan; twenty-two grandchildren; and so many others who call you friend here tonight.

Looking at Dad, I closed:

> Thank you. Yes, thanks for the many accolades, championships won in competition, but mostly how you went about it. How you lived your life and continue to live your life. You are the man, the father I aspire to be. I must say, the last two days I will cherish. To walk Cypress Point and Pebble Beach with Dad and family, so special. I know how blessed we are to have Mom and Dad with us here today.
>
> As we played Cypress Point and we finished the beautiful 16th hole, getting ready to tee off the 17th tee, there's a plaque there that is called Boney's Pulpit. This says so much. And I quote, "Gentlemen, I suggest that we pause for a moment, admire the beautiful view, count our blessings. Very few of us are privileged to pass this way."

I offered another speech that also focused on what Dad's legacy was really all about.

In 2015 Dad received the Congressional Gold Medal, one of the highest civilian awards in the United States. As one of the featured speakers at the presentation in Washington, I told the crowd, "No name is more synonymous with greatness in the sport of golf than the name Jack Nicklaus. Jack Nicklaus is the man.

I believe he has truly transcended the game of golf, and perhaps sports in general."

Honestly, I didn't think I was up to the task when Dad asked me to speak. In fact, I asked Dad if he wanted one of his peers, maybe his good friend Tom Watson, to introduce him. When Arnold Palmer was presented his Congressional Gold Medal in 2012, Dad introduced him. I knew how overwhelming it would be for me to introduce Dad, and I didn't know if I could do a good job. Trying to be funny, Dad smiled and told me to consider it practice for his eulogy.

That didn't make it any easier for me, but here is what I said:

> To share some of my clarity with you, let's go back [to] a time in sports history that many of us remember, the '86 Masters. We've heard about it earlier, but I will tell it from a little bit different perspective.
>
> It was a beautiful spring day in Augusta, Georgia. It was Masters Sunday. I was a twenty-four-year-old kid carrying the bag for Dad. We were on the 9th green, and Dad had just backed away for the second time from a slippery downhill birdie putt. There had been back-to-back roars from the 8th green, where Tom Kite and Seve Ballesteros had each made eagles to extend their leads. I stood with the gallery there on the 9th green. There was a tension in the air. We were caught up in the moment of nervous energies of golf history. It was a moment that seemed to swallow us, all of us, except Dad.
>
> Unexpectedly, Dad turned to the surrounding gallery, flashed a boyish grin, and said in his high-pitched voice with a certain level of levity, "Hey, let's see if we can make some noise of our own up here." He then steadied himself at the task at

hand, as he walked that putt into the hole, the crowd erupted, the game was on.

It was that final nine holes that is forever etched in my memory. I remember that fluid yet powerful swing. I remember the precision, the concentration, the intensity. I remember each heroic putt, each heroic shot. Above all, I remember the emotions. Dad clearly had a mission to give everything he had left. To manage the only thing he could truly manage, himself.

Yet I watched him struggle. I can still see the tears in his eyes and feel those in mine. It was the encouragement and the ovations the fans gave Dad those final nine holes that was unforgettable. Sure, the enthusiasm was fueled by the events of that day, but I knew it was more than that. The cheers represented an appreciation for a lifetime of accomplishments and the way he had done it. They embraced a good man with good character.

Dad was now on the 18th green. I stood motionless, holding the flag, as Dad putted out for a final round 65 to complete his unlikely come-from-behind victory at the age of forty-six. As his final putt dropped, the crowd erupted. Dad quickly picked the ball from the cup and faced the crowd to greet their cheers.

And there I was, completing the mundane task of placing the flag back into the cup. For me, time was standing still as the cheers continued. I was thinking, *Wow, Dad really played great today*. Yet it was more, so much more. This man, this wonderful man, had accomplished so much. He is Jack Nicklaus; he is arguably the greatest golfer in the history of golf. The Golden Bear had just won his sixth green jacket in incredible fashion. His fans adored him. It was his moment in time. A moment so earned and a moment so deserved.

Now, let's go back to that question that I am so often asked: What is it like to be Jack Nicklaus's son?

So there I was, turning from the flag, and all I saw was my dad. In the midst of this moment—that was all about Jack Nicklaus—there Dad stood, waiting for me with the most wonderful smile. His arms were outstretched to embrace me. Dad had made me a part of it. I knew I had Dad's full focus. I felt like I mattered. And I felt loved. That is what it's like to be his son.[1]

The envelope came to my house, and in it was a handwritten note in black felt pen. It was dated March 29—five days after the presentation. It said:

> Dear Son,
>
> What can I say except that I am so proud of you and what you said Tuesday in Washington. Your talk was so good that I didn't care what I said. You made your father one happy and lucky man. To know he has a son as great as you. You are the best!!!
>
> Love you,
>
> Dad

Over the years Dad has played golf with four presidents: Gerald Ford, Bill Clinton, George H. W. Bush, and Donald Trump. One of Dad's fondest conversations among that foursome was one he had with President Clinton following a round of golf. President Clinton said, "Jack, I need some advice."

"Mr. President, I don't know what advice I can give you," Dad replied.

President Clinton explained to Dad that his wife, Hillary, wanted him to meet with a gentleman that afternoon who had donated a large amount of money to his presidential campaign. But their daughter, Chelsea, wanted to go horseback riding. "What should I do?" President Clinton asked Dad.

"Mr. President, that's simple," Dad answered. Continuing, he explained that the gentleman who had donated the money could wait, but Chelsea wouldn't be a teenager much longer. President Clinton made the right decision and took his daughter horseback riding.

Most of us will never sit in the White House, but all of us can learn an important lesson here. Our children are our true legacies, and we should spend as much time as possible with them. There will always be other demands on our time and attention. But, as my dad reminded President Clinton, your time with them as children is limited.

CHAPTER 12

Be Prepared So You're Mentally Tough

Millions of people have had the opportunity through attendance at tournaments or watching on television to see Dad perform over the four days of any golf tournament. Almost none of them, though, had the chance to see what really made him great. It was the multitude of hours he put in practicing the game and his unique skill set that really led to all those trophies.

There is certainly some physical proof of all that practice. Golf pundits say my dad's classic right-handed golf swing is unmistakable. They point to his hip turn, the lift of his left foot off the ground, and his consistent tempo. Those are just some of the components, practiced often, that helped him win.

What the pundits don't know is that a McDonald's Happy Meal was also part of his success.

Seriously.

Dad missed the cut at the 1988 PGA Championship at Oak Tree Golf Club in Oklahoma. Under normal circumstances, golfers are quick to leave town when they miss the cut and don't advance into the tournament's final two rounds. They don't make money or get paid when that happens, so there's really no reason to stick around.

Dad agreed, however, to help ABC with its telecast of that championship and stayed at the tournament with Mom instead of returning to Florida. I know it had to be tough on Dad because there is nothing worse than missing the cut and having to stick around to watch the competition.

During the third round, while Dad was on the air, Mom took Michael to McDonald's where Michael ordered a Happy Meal and a drink. McDonald's was running a special, and each meal came with a glass that had a Peanuts character offering an inspirational phrase. Michael's glass quoted Lucy saying, "There's no excuse for not being properly prepared." Mom was so taken by the phrase that she brought the glass back to the hotel and had Dad read the saying the next morning. The phrase had a profound effect on Dad, even at age forty-eight. He recognized that he hadn't been prepared for the tournament. For years, Dad had a regimen for course preparation, and he hadn't followed it. Dad had his morning orange juice served in that glass to remind him about the importance of preparation. He and Mom still laugh often about that morning. Incidentally, she still has that Happy Meal glass.

Let me come clean regarding the story of Dad failing to prepare for that PGA Championship. Because of Dad's busy schedule, if we were to plan any big event, we would first have to look at Dad's calendar. I had recently gotten engaged, and we needed a date for the wedding. The only opening in Dad's calendar was the weekend before the PGA Championship. Rather than following typical pre-tournament protocol, Dad (as my best man) was busy keeping me calm as the groom instead of walking the course as he otherwise would have been. It was hard to be well prepared for both—a choice he would gladly make again.

Dad didn't argue.

Dad mapped out his calendar each year by highlighting the major championships. He always felt he needed to be mentally as well as physically prepared for the most important tournaments. That's why Dad usually did not play tournament golf the week before or after a major championship. Typically, he visited the host site of the major the week before to play the course a couple of times. His goal was always to get his work in the week before the event. He would walk the course, study every inch of it, and make notes on a scorecard. This was a tactic Dad learned when he played the 1961 U.S. Amateur, where he paced off his approach shot distances at the suggestion of fellow golfer and future PGA Tour Commissioner Deane Beman.

For example, Dad highlighted the carry distance over a certain bunker from the back of the tee. He'd write down the distance in yards from a sprinkler head in the fairway to the front of the green. Dad's notes on yardage were usually measured to the green fronts. He might add yardage to his calculation if a bunker or water hazard required greater carry on his shot. For example, Dad might note "186 past double tree on rt. (192 over Sh Lt bunker) = sprinkler head." Most of us would look at those notes as gibberish. For Dad, the notes he recorded served as a roadmap for how he intended to play each hole. For instance, with this note he located a sprinkler head just past two large oak trees, right of the fairway. He walked and recorded that it was 186 yards from the sprinkler head to the front of the green. If there was a bunker front left greenside, he would record the additional yardage to carry that bunker.

As his caddie, I would go out the morning of a tournament with those notes and make sure all the distances were correct. I would also pace and record every green's pin location, which is changed each day by the greenskeeper. Those calculations were a key part of Dad's preparation and helped ensure he was ready for a tournament.

Being prepared doesn't always mean you will win. And Dad never made excuses when he didn't. That was never more evident than when Dad lost by one stroke to Tom Watson in the 1977 Open Championship in Turnberry, Scotland, a tournament remembered as the "Duel in the Sun." After Dad made a thirty-five-foot birdie putt on the 18th hole to pull even, Tom sank a two-foot putt for his seventh birdie of the round and the victory. As Dad and Tom shook hands, Dad put his arm around Tom and said, "Tom, I gave you my best shot, and it wasn't good enough."

Tom replied, "Hearing that from you was amazing."

With all the preparation he put in, Dad knew he was ready to compete. So even though Tom had prevailed that Sunday afternoon, Dad felt good about his preparation and performance. He had left it all on the course.

Five years later, at the 1982 U.S. Open in Pebble Beach, Tom also executed one of the most famous shots in golf history—coined "the Chip Shot Heard 'Round the World"—at Dad's expense. They were tied for the lead when Tom hit his tee shot on the par-3 17th over the green into the long, thick rough. With the ball about sixteen feet uphill from the hole, the shot looked impossible. But Tom executed an incredible shot that hit the flag stick and dropped into the hole.

After Tom won the tournament, Dad wrapped his left arm around Tom in congratulations. "You did it to me again," Dad said. "I am really proud and happy for you." Everyone standing nearby could sense how genuine Dad was. When asked by reporters later about the conversation, Tom said, "That was typical Jack Nicklaus: the epitome of what a champion should be."[1] Once again Dad came into the tournament fully prepared, but it was not enough to beat Tom. Even though Dad fell short, it was an incredible moment. When you and your opponent come fully prepared, competition can bring out the best in both of you and take your game to the next level.

Dad always said being better prepared made him mentally tougher than his opponents. He often found a way to win because he would almost never beat himself, which also was an offshoot of Dad's preparation.

While I understood the importance of mental toughness on the golf course, I was surprised the first time I heard Dad's perspective on it. Dad and I played together in a two-man tournament years ago at Thanksgiving Point, a course in Lehi, Utah, near Salt Lake City, designed by Hall of Fame pro golfer and former NBC golf analyst Johnny Miller. I always loved how candid Johnny was on television, but some of the pros criticized him when he described some of his fellow golfers who choked under pressure playing the game.

After the event in Utah, we flew to Jackson Hole to fish. One day while in the car with Dad, Ken Leister, a business partner with Miller, asked, "How is it you never seem to choke?" Dad, who was driving, didn't hesitate and answered, "Because I am not afraid to win."

I was in the back seat listening and chimed in, "Don't you mean you aren't afraid to lose?"

Dad quickly corrected me.

"No," he said. "I'm not afraid to win. Anyone can lose. It's easy. But it takes courage to win. Because when you win, you separate yourself from your competitors. You become the standard."

Dad had no problem being the standard.

I had countless opportunities to interact with golfers during tournaments when I caddied for my dad. I was on Dad's bag in the late 1980s at the Memorial Tournament, where he was paired with Fuzzy Zoeller in the final round. As we walked in the fairway of the 9th hole, Fuzzy pulled me aside and said, "Jackie, this is fun."

I asked Fuzzy what he meant, and he said, "I've played with your dad a few times when he gets into this mode, this trance, this gear. Whatever you want to call it, he goes to a different place than any of us can. But whatever it is, it's a different gear he switches to."

I was taken aback. This was his competitor telling me this as we walked along—how much he enjoyed watching my dad lock in.

Fuzzy continued, "Jackie, he's in that gear right now. I know I'm supposed to be competing with him, but frankly, I'm sitting back and watching it because this is so much fun." I took Fuzzy's advice that day and for every day forward—remembering to sit back and watch my dad because I had a great seat. Fuzzy was right. I approached Dad and handed him his 6-iron. He choked down on the club and hit it stiff, a frozen rope that stopped three feet from the pin. He made a birdie.

Fuzzy tugged on my arm, smiled, and said, "See what I told you. Just sit back and enjoy. This is fun."

It was. It still is.

Children—even my kids when they were young—will sometimes cry when they don't do well in an athletic event. As a parent, my father taught me to respond by asking, "Did you try your best? Did you put your best foot forward?" And if I couldn't answer yes to those two questions, he would encourage me to come back the next day and work to be ready for the next competition. "Come back and be better prepared," Dad would say. That was something my kids heard over and over again growing up—and it applies to all of us. No matter how good you are at a specific task or skill, you can always do better.

But this lesson doesn't come with fanfare and adulation. "Put in the work when the lights are off and nobody is watching," Dad said.

It certainly worked for him.

CHAPTER 13

Show Faith Through Actions, Not Just Words

"Preach the gospel at all times. Use words if necessary." It's reported that Saint Francis of Assisi said those words when asked by others how a person should express his faith. And while most who know me wouldn't expect me to pull out a supposedly eight-hundred-year-old quote from a Catholic friar, when I heard the words, I thought immediately of Dad. He is the living example of those words.

Clearly my father always had faith in himself, but the faith he would tell you was more important to his success was his faith in God. It wasn't a discussion he had with reporters; it has always been his—and our family's—take on faith to keep this portion of our lives rather private. Within our house, believing in our Creator was a central part of our life and success, and I'm sure no one who has spent time with Dad would question his faith. The lesson that both my parents taught us as their children mirrors exactly the way I've shared the discussion regarding faith with my children.

As I was writing this book, the importance of faith and how it was taught led to a great discussion with both of my parents. "Believing in Christ was just a way of life," Mom said.

Then Dad summed it up. "I thought it was important to teach you about God the same way I taught you golf," he said rather matter-of-factly. "Go through and make sure you understand the importance and the fundamentals, then let each of you come to decisions based on what you saw, not what you might think was being forced. If the decision becomes truly yours, the impact will be far greater. My father and mother taught faith to me, basically, the same way."

Mom and Dad passed that faith on to us, one of the greatest gifts they ever gave us. And as a Christ-follower today, I know the way Mom and Dad set the example worked for me.

As often as she could, Mom made sure she and the five kids attended our Methodist church and Sunday school and learned about God and Jesus. She said she made it a point for us to sit in the front row so none of us would be tempted to nod off or misbehave.

We didn't attend church every Sunday because as a family we traveled to Dad's golf tournaments many weekends. Dad got to go to church far less frequently than we did. He worked on Sunday. (At least he hoped every week to be working on Sunday!) But Dad made the point that a church attendance roster was no way to define our relationship with God. Of the five children I probably traveled more with Dad than the others. I first caddied for Dad when I was fourteen years old and was on his golf bag many weekends as a teenager and beyond, missing many Sundays at home.

PGA Tour players compete in twenty to thirty tournaments annually—Dad played in 586 PGA Tour events during his forty-three-year career. He traveled nationally and internationally, making pew appearances nearly impossible. On the tour, several players have, for many years, made it a point to gather for a group Bible study on Sunday mornings. Dad didn't attend those gatherings, choosing to make his private time of worship his own. He read and prayed. But he did it alone.

Dad thought of the golf course as his place to witness. When he was out there, the crowds were watching. In his mind it wouldn't have mattered what he did on Sunday mornings if on Sunday afternoons he cursed and acted in ways that would have dishonored his Lord. Similarly, it wouldn't matter how many times you pointed toward heaven after a great putt if you disrespected your wife and family through your actions or words. Many people can put on a good show in public. But your core, who you truly are, is defined by what happens when nobody is watching.

I have tried to instill my parents' commitment to faith in my kids through many of the same ways. I believed the way they watched a Christian life lived would help set an example, and I am proud of the direction each of them has chosen.

One of the most important teachings in the Bible is the admonition that each of us must love our neighbor. I know there's a chapter ahead in this book on my parents' work for charitable organizations, but as I think about how my father and mother lived their faith, I think about many of the little ways they showed love to neighbors.

Dad would often encourage us, as children, to find little ways to help people. The greatest lesson in what he was teaching, though, was the importance of showing empathy for others, of not being judgmental of circumstances we might not understand.

You never know what other people are going through in their lives. Even a small interaction when passing someone on a sidewalk can entirely change a person's day. Being respectful, appreciative, kind, caring, and listening to and learning from your friends, family, and strangers is very important. As big as our world is, it truly is small.

And in those moments, you may be opening a heart.

While I learned the key elements of Christian faith in Sunday school and at home, my understanding of the Lord grew deeper during the years I played high school football at the Benjamin School. Our coaching staff was filled with men of faith, and they never hesitated to share their commitment. Every Wednesday night during the football season, I was one of eight players who went to Coach Ron Ream's home for Bible study. We read Bible verses and then discussed what we thought a passage meant and how we thought God intended it to impact our lives.

Of course, as teenagers, there were other reasons that motivated us to attend those sessions. Coach Ream's wife, Linda, made sure every evening ended with bowls of ice cream. We were baited! I'm a little embarrassed to admit it, but back then the ice cream was a pretty significant draw. We thought the chief reward of those meetings was satisfying our sweet tooth. It would take years for us to fully grasp, but our reward was far deeper and much more meaningful in becoming closer to God.

Before every football game, Coach Tom Mullins, our offensive coordinator, led our team in prayer. With our eyes closed and heads bowed, we prayed for safety and support, a meaningful and important pregame practice. Then, as a team, we recited the Lord's Prayer.

We learned football too, and the coaches, along with head coach Mickey Neal, did a powerful job of connecting elements of faith to what the sport was teaching us. We went 21–3 my junior and senior seasons, with two of the defeats coming in the state finals. During those special years, my teammates and I learned the importance of teamwork, sportsmanship, how to win, and how to handle a loss. We also learned the true meaning of "I have your back." Football is unlike any other sport because, no matter how good you are, you will get knocked on your tail. Often. But you need to get up and line up again. Sounds a lot like life, huh? And how you relate to your faith helps you pick yourself up. Those coaches remain such a great influence in my life to this day. I learned so much from them, from learning the Bible to playing football—and through them I learned a valuable lesson about faith from my father.

Coach Mullins would go on to found and pastor Christ Fellowship Church, a nondenominational multisite church. What started in 1984 as a small Bible study in Tom and Donna's living room has grown to be one of the largest churches in America. Based in Palm Beach Gardens, the church operates eight other campuses across Palm Beach County, serving tens of thousands of people in Southeast Florida.

Dad actually played a role in Coach Mullins's decision to start the church.

Dad and Tom were playing tennis one afternoon when Coach mentioned that he felt he hadn't fulfilled God's intentions. Dad encouraged Coach to "go for it. All of us who know you know that's what you always wanted to do." And Tom did.

Tom resigned from his job as the athletic director at Palm Beach State College to pursue the ministry full-time. Over the years, Tom wrote books and traveled internationally with Donna on behalf of world-renowned organizations, including Campus Crusade for Christ. Tom and Donna founded Place of Hope Children's Home and Place of Hope International Children's Homes.

Dad felt good that he helped propel a person toward full-time ministry. Sometimes a person just needs a little push to chase their destiny. Just like we need to have faith in God, we also need to have faith to step out of a comfortable job to pursue something like a ministry.

While going to church when growing up created a foundation, and attending Bible studies with high school football coaches built on that foundation, it was while I was playing golf at the University of North Carolina that I fully committed myself to Christ.

As a freshman at UNC, I was required, like all freshmen athletes, to attend study hall four nights a week. Early on I became close to a quarterback on the football team, Scott Stankavage. Faith was an important part of Scott's life, and you couldn't help but be impressed by the way he carried himself. Scott loved all sports, particularly basketball, and we often found ourselves teaming up during pickup games. Occasionally another freshman—a forward on the basketball team named Matt Doherty—joined in. (Matt would go on to win a national championship with some guy named Jordan and, for a short while, coach at UNC.)

Scott and I spoke about faith a number of times, and he encouraged me to get to know Mike Echstenkamper, the campus leader from the Fellowship of Christian Athletes. Mike and I ended up grabbing lunch a few times, and after one of those meals we were on a walk around campus and ended up in the famous home of Tar Heel basketball, Carmichael Arena, sitting up in the stands, just the two of us.

"Jackie, have you ever actually prayed and asked Christ into your life?" Mike asked.

"Actually, no," I said, realizing I had learned a lot growing up but never actually said the words.

"Well, if this is the right time for you, there's no better time to than now," he said.

I didn't hesitate, bowing my head as he led me through the sinner's prayer, as it is called, asking Christ to become my Savior. Almost immediately it felt as if a huge weight was lifted from my shoulders. I don't know any other way to describe it but to use that phrase. It wasn't just a mental lift, it was physical. I got up and felt I was lighter physically.

Mike and FCA became an important piece of my growth over my years in Chapel Hill. I also went a few times to church with Scott after that, though his Catholic faith was a little hard for me to connect with. After that, Scott and I spent a lot of time sitting in his room or my room, reading Bible verses and relating what we were reading to life. Scott had a big influence on my life and my thinking. And, because of him, I began a relationship with Christ that changed everything for me from that day forward.

CHAPTER 14

Be Helpful but Keep the Competitive Fires Burning

It's pretty easy to imagine when you live your life with someone considered the Greatest of All Time (GOAT) at something, that the most important lessons in competitiveness would come from the GOAT.

But in our house, the GOAT's wife could teach you a thing or two on this subject as well. Mom has learned how to compete in her more than sixty years of living with Dad.

Mom came from a conservative family in Ohio and is a sweet, sweet lady who has helped everyone, and I mean everyone, over the years. She has such a kind voice and nature that most would never believe that hidden below all that goodness is . . . a trash-talker!

My parents love to fish together, and early in their marriage, Mom would giggle quietly if she caught a bigger fish than Dad. But over the course of sixty years the giggling has become some pretty impressive trash talking. And there's nothing funnier than listening to sweet Barbara talk smack. These two, both in their eighties, have spent entire days on the water in a sixteen-foot flat boat. They have literally baked in the sun in the Bahamas, in the Florida Keys, or on the water near our house in their quest to land the biggest fish. The boat is stocked with lunch, water, and plenty of competitive juice.

They love to catch bonefish with fly rods, a method that features a lightweight lure (called an artificial fly) and requires a fair amount of skill to cast. The water is crystal clear and shallow enough to where either the boat is slowly pushed across the water with a long pole or Mom and Dad are able to walk along the sandy bottom. Their setup must be timed perfectly when a bonefish is spotted because the average casting distance is twenty-five to thirty feet. The average bonefish weighs between three and five pounds (the Florida record is sixteen pounds), and it can grow to as long as three feet. The fish is vulnerable in shallow water as it feeds or tries to stay hidden from sharks.

When a bonefish hits the hook, it usually takes off for deeper waters. And that's when the fun starts. It can accelerate to an average speed of forty miles per hour and, for its size, puts up a tremendous fight. Once the bonefish is reeled to the boat, Mom and Dad estimate its length and weight, release it—and then they do it all over again! It could be one hundred degrees without any shade, but Mom and Dad have stayed out there all day, trading positions on the boat's bow. And keeping score. Because it's not just fishing, it's a competition.

According to Mom, she started feeling a little comfortable showing her competitive fire with Dad during a fishing trip to the Bahamas nearly twenty years ago. Mom had been used to spin-fishing and using bait, but Dad was helping her learn how to fly-fish. Dad was trying to be the great teacher he is and was offering lots of suggestions. Then, by day's end, the biggest fish belonged to . . . Mom!

Mom said she didn't say anything about having the big prize, but later that evening "Dad was pouting." Now, Dad denies that he was pouting—his line was "I don't pout; I get even." When Mom pointed out at dinner that Dad seemed to have his feelings hurt, he mumbled something about the biggest fish. Mom jumped all over the moment. "Yeah, I did catch the biggest fish," she said. "And I intend to do it every time."

A couple of other moments that still stick in Dad's craw came while they were trout fishing in Utah and then bonefishing off the coast of Christmas Island.

During the Utah trip, Mom and Dad were out on a river, separated by fifty yards or so, and they were fly-fishing, using essentially the same equipment. After a bit, Dad called to Mom to see how she was doing.

"I've caught eleven," Mom replied. "What about you?"

Dad didn't answer. He had caught only one. "Ridiculous" was the only word he used to describe the situation. "She was using the same fly."

"Don't worry," Mom said in her most patronizing voice. "It looks like you're doing everything right."

When they were on Christmas Island—an external territory of Australia—a couple of years later, they were in shallow water, walking a flat, bonefishing. Mom was accompanied by a fishing guide named Tanaka, but on this particular day the guide didn't have to help much. Mom was on fire. She was catching fish one after the other while Dad, standing just thirty yards away, was stuck on two.

Mom giggled, looked at Dad, and offered, "You want to come take my place over here?" The ultimate insult.

"No, I don't want your place over there," Dad snapped. Nothing more was said.

Fishing has become a wonderful way for the two of them to get out together, enjoy the sun, and compete. When I asked Dad about Mom's trash-talking, he agreed that she doesn't needle all the time, but when she does, she's good at it. "The worst is when she offers, 'You want to use my rod and my fly?'" Dad said.

I should have just kept my mouth shut.

Nope.

Trash-talking might have worked for Mom, but it never helped me, particularly on the golf course against the GOAT.

The goal of every child is to beat his or her father, right? That was particularly true for me against Dad. My younger brother Gary and I always competed against each other, but our real desire was to beat Dad on the golf course. We played together countless times on our home course, Lost Tree Club in Florida, and at Muirfield Village in Ohio. Gary beat Dad on the golf course for the first time when he was fifteen. I beat Dad for the first time when I was sixteen or seventeen.

My apologies, but not every golfer is a gracious gentleman. (Spoiler alert: me!) I should have known better than to poke the Golden Bear. It only awakened the competitor in him. When I caddied for Dad on the PGA Tour, his fellow players told me the last thing they wanted to do was get Dad riled up. They never pointed to the scoreboard when Dad trailed.

I didn't learn that lesson. I talked trash, and it seldom worked to my benefit.

If we were playing and I had the lead with three or four holes left, I couldn't help myself.

"Dad, I've got you by a shot."

"Dad, I am beating you."

"Dad, I am tied with you."

Why I ever said a word was beyond me. Invariably, Dad would quietly one-putt the final three greens. He'd go birdie, birdie, birdie and beat me by two shots. That was Dad's way of talking trash. It was important to Dad that he made us work to beat him. He was not the father handing out the participation trophies. He always played with blinders on when it came to playing golf with his sons. We had to earn it. There weren't any mulligans (extra shots) or gimme putts (stroke counts without being played) when the Nicklaus family showed up to play.

I was still playing professionally and in my early twenties when I was partnered with Dad for a round at the Memorial Tournament. I'm not sure what year it was, but Dad had finished on the cut line and an uneven number of players in the field advanced. Since the round featured twosomes, Dad needed a playing partner and asked me. Even though I was only playing alongside my father and was not competing in the tournament, I was honored, but nervous, because I had never played in front of galleries that large and under a spotlight that bright.

Since Dad and I were the first twosome off the tee, we served as the pacesetters for the golfers behind us. We had to play relatively fast to ensure a good flow behind us. I got off to a nice start. We got to the 6th hole, and I was 2 under par. Dad, on the other hand, was 2 over.

This time I kept my mouth shut. I was probably too nervous to say anything, but I knew I was playing well. As we walked off the 6th green, I will never forget Dad said, "You know what? We are not out here to shoot a score. We are out here to be pacesetters. Come on, let's hurry up, let's get moving."

Now I was even more nervous. Sure, I was just playing golf with Dad, but my dad was Jack Nicklaus. This was his arena. And he wanted us to pick up the pace.

On the 7th tee, I hit a duck-hook into the woods. I bogeyed the hole while Dad birdied it. Now I was 1 under par, and Dad was 1 over par. I bogeyed the next hole to fall to even; Dad parred to remain 1 over. Then I double-bogeyed No. 9 while Dad birdied. So in the span of three holes, I went from a four-stroke lead over Dad to a two-stroke deficit. All this happened after Dad told me to hurry up. I bet you can see where this is going. But wait, it actually gets better.

As we walked to the 10th tee, Dad put his arm around me and said, as serious as he could be, "You know what? All these people out here, they really came to watch a show. Why don't we give them a show? Let's just slow down and enjoy this."

Dad won't admit it, but he was clearly messing with my head. He knew I was whipping him! He knew he wasn't playing well, so he wanted to play fast. That disrupted any rhythm or confidence I might have had. But then when he started to play well, it was time to slow down. And that messed with my head even further. Dad beat me by a couple of shots, but that was still a big moment for me. He has always been Dad—and always will be Dad regardless of how he's doing—but that's another example of how he puts his blinders on when there's an opportunity to compete.

Despite Dad's fierce competitiveness, he was also more than happy to offer advice to fellow players on the PGA Tour. He never had a problem with it. Dad has always felt golf, and sports in general, lends itself to helping and mentoring people—even if those people might show up the next day as your competitor.

That happened at the 1964 St. Petersburg Open Invitational in St. Petersburg, Florida, where Dad and Bruce Devlin were among the leaders heading into Sunday's final round. Bruce struggled off the tee in Saturday's third round, so Dad helped him for about an hour after the round on the practice tee. Guess what? Bruce won the tournament by four strokes. Dad tipped his cap to Bruce and went back to work on his own game in preparation for the next tournament.

Dad believes today's golfers would be willing to help each other, though he thinks player entourages and egos make those gestures more difficult. To this day he makes himself available for sessions with tour players from bright stars to up-and-comers.

One of the first young golfers who reached out to Dad for advice was Australia's Aaron Baddeley, who turned professional in 2000 and, by 2020, had twelve career wins on three tours (the PGA Tour, the European Tour, and the PGA Tour of Australasia). Aaron and Dad, who was still playing on the PGA Champions Tour at the time, met for lunch in Palm Beach and talked about Aaron's game and the importance of mental preparation.

Timing is everything, right? South African Trevor Immelman sought out Dad's advice over lunch prior to the 2008 Masters Tournament. Trevor picked Dad's brain on the best way to play Augusta National. Trevor then went on to win the Masters by three strokes over favorite Tiger Woods to claim his first win in a major. Fellow South African Charl Schwartzel sought out Dad's advice prior to the 2011 Masters and went on to win in Augusta that year by two strokes over Adam Scott and Jason Day. Charl was the third South African winner of the event after Dad's good friend Gary Player, and Trevor, three years earlier.

Wanting to know more about the Muirfield Village golf course, American Patrick Cantlay and Dad talked about how to play the course prior to the 2018 Memorial Tournament. Patrick filed that advice away and won the Memorial a year later.

One of the best golfers in the world is Rory McIlroy, who has spent more than one hundred weeks in the top spot of the Official World Golf Ranking. Only three players—Dad, Tiger Woods, and Rory—have won four majors by the age of twenty-five.

Rory, who was born in Northern Ireland and lives in Jupiter, Florida, turned professional at age seventeen. In 2008 Rory met with Dad to discuss how to finish tournaments when you are in contention. During his career, Dad was known as one of the best finishers in golf. During Dad's rookie season on the PGA Tour in 1962, he won three tournaments, had sixteen top-ten finishes in twenty-six tournaments (including three second-place finishes), and was named the tour's Rookie of the Year.

Dad and Rory talked about the importance of being patient, playing within yourself, how winning breeds winning, and building on your experiences, both good and bad.

Dad has always believed most golf tournaments are not won on one particular shot. However, they can be lost on one shot if a golfer is not careful. Dad feels there are times to be patient and times to be aggressive. Another key component is to play within yourself and know what you can and can't do on each shot. Of all the skill and qualities needed on the golf course, Dad believes patience has to emerge as a strength to be successful.

When Rory won the 2010 Quail Hollow Championship, he shot a final-round 62 to beat Phil Mickelson by four strokes. Rory's final round set a new course record, and he became the first player since Tiger Woods to win a PGA Tour event prior to his twenty-first birthday. Dad told Rory, "I told you to be patient, but this is ridiculous."

Rory learned a tough but valuable lesson at the 2011 Masters Tournament. He shot an opening-round 7-under-par 65 to become the youngest player at the time to lead the Masters on the first day. Rory carried the lead into Sunday's final round, but he shot what was the worst round (80) in history by any professional golfer leading after the third round in the Masters. As a result, Rory finished tied for fifteenth in the tournament.

When Dad and Rory spoke a few months later, Dad asked him, "Did you learn anything? Did you learn why you did that? There was no use having that experience if you didn't learn why you did it."

Rory answered, "I think I did. I think I learned why I did that and why it happened to me."

Dad said, "Well, you have the U.S. Open coming up, so apply what you learned. And make the loss worth it."

Two months later Rory applied it in a big way. He won his first major championship at the U.S. Open at Congressional in Bethesda, Maryland, by eight strokes over Jason Day. He finished 16 under par in the tournament and set a bunch of tournament records, including a 72-hole total of 268 to shatter the previous record held by . . . Dad. Dad set that record in Baltursol in 1980.

Dad dropped a note to Rory:

Congratulations. You obviously learned something from your Augusta experience. But, more important, did you learn anything from the experience of winning, and why you won?

You learned why you lost. Did you learn why you won?

Imagine getting a note like that from a guy who has won eighteen majors. That's who Dad is.

Dad learned how to break down wins and losses early in his career. Over the years, however, Dad also realized he didn't always listen to his own advice, specifically when it came to patience. The two best examples are the 15th hole at Augusta National and the 18th green at Pebble Beach Golf Links.

In 1971 Dad finished second in the Masters by two strokes, largely due to a triple-bogey 8 he carded on the 15th hole. Dad was way too aggressive with his approach shot from 250-plus yards, dumping consecutive shots into the water in front of the green.

The following year—even though Dad led the Masters from wire to wire for his fourth win—he faced the same exact shot on the same hole, this time into the wind. He cranked a 3-wood that barely cleared the water and landed in the front of the green. In 2017, when Dad watched Golf Channel's documentary on him, titled *Jack*, it featured that shot from forty-five years earlier. Dad burst out in laughter. On that 15th hole he knew full well he'd done the exact opposite of what he had preached to golfers about being patient and playing within yourself.

In the early 1960s at the Bing Crosby National Pro-Am

Tournament at Pebble Beach, Dad needed a birdie on the par-5 18th to win or a par to tie Phil Rogers. Dad hit his third shot about twenty feet behind the hole. Again, Dad was too aggressive and convinced himself he needed to make that putt. He pushed the putt four feet past the hole and also missed the comebacker.

Oh, that was pretty stupid, Dad said to himself when he analyzed his decision. Later he figured he probably had about a 15 percent chance to make that putt but a better than 50 percent chance to win the tournament in a playoff. He vowed never to 3-putt again on the 18th green at Pebble Beach—and he never did.

Dad has always thought that experience is an important key to success. How you carry experiences from one tournament to the next will determine how competitive you will be.

Other golfers who have reached out to Dad over the years include Justin Thomas, Dustin Johnson, Rickie Fowler, Daniel Berger, and Patrick Rogers. Dad told me that having today's stars reach out to him keeps him connected to the game. "If I didn't really know any of the players out there, I might not watch some of these tournaments. But I am lucky to have gotten to know them."

It might sound odd, but Dad is flattered when approached for advice. While writing this book, we talked about the advice he has given to so many. He smiled. "How many children listen to their parents? Or listen to their grandparents? In these conversations it feels like someone is listening to me."

As he said that, I had to plead guilty. I was the kid who once said his dad knew nothing about golf!

During Dad's early days on the PGA Tour, he credited Arnold Palmer and Gary Player, among others, for taking the time to help him. Another person who played an even larger role was a name you might not recognize: Joe Black. Joe played on the PGA Tour for a short period but became more successful as the tournament supervisor on the tour staff. Joe was considered a rules expert and served as chairman on the rules committee at major tournaments. He also managed the scoring tent behind the 18th green for many years at the Masters.

Joe preached to Dad about being patient. He said, "Jack, instead of shooting 35 or 36 in the last round, one day you will shoot 32, and all of a sudden, 'Oh, hey, look what's here.' A win."

Dad felt that was sound advice, and he always remembered it. To this day, patience is the virtue he passes on to golfers who seek out his advice: play within yourself, be smart, and don't blow the tournament by trying to rush a shot.

Dad has always believed most golf courses have about six difficult-to-make shots. He points to Augusta National as an example: the tee shot at No. 2, the second shot at No. 11, the tee shot on No. 12, the tee shot *and* second shot at No. 13, and the second shot at No. 15 are the shots that can ruin a round. "If you play those shots smart, the rest of the golf course isn't hard," Dad says.

A question my father often gets is how he would compete against Tiger Woods and some of today's young stars. Some say you can't compare different players from different eras because so much has changed within the game over the years. But there's one spot where I know my dad would stand eye-to-eye with any player of any generation. And that is in his passion to compete.

The differences between today's pros and when Dad competed are many.

Prize Money. Dad has said he's envious that today's players can make an incredible living playing golf. Players in Dad's era had to win tournaments to cash checks big enough to support a family. Dad made just under $5.8 million in his forty-three-year career on the PGA Tour, and his winner's check for the 1963 PGA Championship (his first PGA) was $13,000. In 1989 Dad established a personal record in total worldwide winnings for the year with $524,232. In 2019 Brooks Koepka won $9.7 million. The winner of the 2020 Tour Championship was Dustin Johnson, who was handed a check for $15 million.

Equipment. Dad has also acknowledged the advances in golf equipment over the years and has advocated changes to limit how equipment has altered the game. Known as one of the longest drivers of his day, Dad points out that early in his career most drives were in the 220- to 230-yard range. Now, many professionals and amateurs can easily drive beyond three hundred yards. Dad believes the gargantuan driving distance is shrinking golf courses (by yardage) and making some obsolete.

Course Design. Golf courses are getting longer to compensate. Sometimes longer isn't always harder. And if all course designers are doing is adding yardage, they are not really making the game better.

But for all these differences between eras, let me promise you that if you put Dad on the same first tee, they would still be calling him the GOAT.

Whether it was raising his children or offering advice to

today's players, Dad has always been able to balance his competitive spirit with helping other players succeed. Always striving to be the best golfer in the world, Dad also tried to help some of his rivals improve. He knew that having the other players at their best elevated his game. There is a lesson here. We should always be fiercely competitive and doing everything as best as we can even while we help other people succeed. While seemingly at odds, competition and helping others both bring out the best in us.

Mom and Dad's wedding day,
July 23, 1960

Wearing my dad's golf
hat is the best!

Dad, Mom, and me—obviously
excited that he beat Arnold
Palmer in the 1962 U.S. Open,
Dad's first major championship

Dad holding the 1962 U.S. Open trophy, and his father, my
Grandpa Charlie, with the hardware from the 1961 U.S. Amateur

Not wanting Dad to leave
but letting him go so
he could win the 1963
Masters, his first of six

Not a one-sport family—
you can't catch me!

Me with Mom and Grandpa
Charlie in the early 1960s

My favorite place in the world—
Dad's arms—at the 1963 World
Series of Golf, Firestone
Country Club, Akron, Ohio

Me and Steve supporting
Dad's alma mater,
The Ohio State University

A 1965 family photo—not sure what
my brother Steve is planning to do

Me fishing with Dad
in Zanesfield, Ohio,
September 1966

Steve and me honing our
golf skills—a dangerous
adventure for Dad, I'm sure!

A painting of me and
Dad playing in the
swimming pool

Play day in October 1967: Mom, Nan, Steve, me, and Dad

Me tagging along on a goose hunt and allowed to pull the trigger for the first time . . . falling back into Dad's arms

Me listening to Dad speak with President Nixon after Dad won the 1972 U.S. Open at Pebble Beach

Steve and me under Dad's watchful eyes at Lost Tree Club, North Palm Beach, Florida

My first time caddying on the big stage: the 1976 British Open at the Royal Birkdale Golf Club

A 1978 Nicklaus family photo at Muirfield Village Golf Club, Dublin, Ohio: Steve, Mom, Michael, Nan, Dad, Gary, and me

Dad and his boys: me, Michael, Gary, and Steve

One big fish—a 624-pound bluefin tuna—caught off the Cat Cays in the Bahamas, 1984

Dad and me at the August 1986 Jerry Ford Invitational, Vail, Colorado, at the Country Club of the Rockies course, Arrowhead

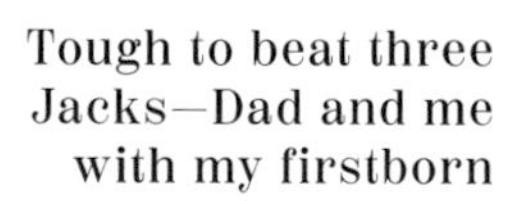

Tough to beat three Jacks—Dad and me with my firstborn

A 2010 family photo: me, Nan, Gary, Mom, Michael, Dad, and Steve

Steve, Dad, Michael, and me at Cypress Point Club, Pebble Beach, California, June 2017

My nephew Jake Walter Nicklaus, forever in our hearts

Family time in 2017—blue skies, bright smiles, and warm hearts: me and Alli, Christie and Casey, Will, Jack and Charlie

Me and Alli at the Pebble Beach home of Jim and Courtney Nantz, June 2017, for "The Calling," a fundraiser for the Nantz National Alzheimer Center

Family photo from Christie and Todger's wedding, December 2020: me, Alli, Charlie, the bride and groom, Casey, Jack, and Will

Mom and Dad, happily married for more than sixty years, continuing to bless and encourage all who know them

CHAPTER 15

Be Ready to Seize Unexpected Opportunities

While I certainly never planned on it, caddying for my dad presented an amazing way to learn more from him as he offered lessons about the game of golf and, more important, about life.

The first time I ever caddied for my dad was at the Open Championship at Royal Birkdale Golf Club in Southport, England, in 1976. It wasn't by plan or design.

Dad's regular Open Championship caddie was Englishman Jimmy Dickinson. Jimmy, who passed away in 2005 at eighty-one, first caddied for Dad at the Open Championship in 1963. He was on Dad's bag for two of his Open Championship titles (1970 and 1978), and they had a great partnership.

I walked the course with Dad as he played his practice round with Raymond Floyd before Thursday's opening round. On the approach to the 9th hole, Jimmy tore his Achilles tendon and couldn't continue. Jimmy asked me to carry Dad's bag to the 10th tee while he looked for a replacement caddie.

While we waited, Dad looked at me and said, "Why don't

you carry the bag for me on the back nine?" At fourteen years old, I really didn't have time to react or even process what Dad was asking. I certainly did not register how much trust Dad was placing in me. I just grabbed the bag, which probably weighed around fifty pounds, and went to work (so to speak). Dad's drive off the tee landed in the middle of the fairway, followed by a perfectly struck 4-iron that landed on the green about five feet from the pin. I watched the flight of the ball, and it seemed to defy gravity with its height and hang time.

I hoisted Dad's bag over my right shoulder, and we walked side by side down the fairway. Although I had spent so much time with Dad on the golf course, it had not been as a caddie. I was like a deer in the headlights, and I was so overwhelmed. I was only a few minutes into my new gig when Dad quickly reminded me of my new responsibilities. We had walked about thirty feet when Dad stopped and asked me, "Didn't you forget something?"

I was surprised by the question and had no idea what Dad was talking about. I turned and looked back down the fairway, thinking I might have dropped a club or that maybe Raymond Floyd had not hit his approach shot yet. I was confused and looked it. Dad pointed to a small chunk of turf that was bottom-side up in the middle of the fairway behind us.

"You forgot to replace the divot," he said, regarding the green turf displaced by his approach shot.

Having let my new role get the better of me, I was embarrassed as I found the dislodged turf and replaced it. This was "Golf 101," an etiquette rule I knew as a golfer. It was time for me to focus since I was in Dad's office—and this was serious business.

I set Dad's bag down on the fairway, and nobody replaced a

divot quicker or better than I did then. It was the best replaced divot in the history of replacing divots!

Then the nerves surfaced. I was a wreck, worried because Dad said he didn't need a replacement caddie for Jimmy. He had me, and I was wondering whether I was up to the task. Yet, as he always is, Dad was incredible. Honestly, it was hard to believe he played so well—Dad finished in a second-place tie with Seve Ballesteros, six strokes behind winner Johnny Miller. Dad was at a huge disadvantage with an inexperienced son-turned-caddie on his bag. I didn't know anything about being a caddie other than the oft-repeated mantra, "Show up. Keep up. And shut up!"

As Dad's caddie, I had big shoes to fill. Jimmy was well respected and successful, one of the best in the game. When Dad opened Muirfield Village Golf Club in Columbus in 1974—named after Muirfield, Scotland, where Dad won the first of his three Open Championships in 1966—Jimmy served as its first caddie master before he returned to England.

When I caddied that first time for Dad, our relationship changed. He was Dad first and always, but I also quickly understood that he was working when on the course. Golf was his profession, what he did for a living to support his family. Out there I saw him as a competitor for the first time. With me on his bag, I also understood I could help or hurt his performance.

Mom and Dad had to be entertained by my first efforts since I was determined to be the best caddie I could be. And, boy, I overdid it at times.

Like most guys on the PGA Tour, Dad always marked his

golf balls with a pencil mark on either side of the number on the ball. It was something he always did just before he teed his ball up on the first tee of a round. It was a light press of the pencil lead, barely visible, but enough to distinguish it if there was ever a question of golf ball identification.

Dad never marked his golf balls during a practice round. So, after his practice round at the Open Championship, I wanted Dad to be prepared. I marked all the golf balls Dad planned to use in the next day's opening round before we went to bed. At that time balata golf balls were the choice for professionals and low-handicap golfers. The soft balata cover allowed for more control off the tee and much higher spin rates on iron and wedge shots.

I was determined to mark Dad's golf balls like no others. I planned to have the most thorough markings ever on a golf ball. Well, I went through pencil after pencil after pencil as I marked those golf balls. I can't tell you how many tips of pencil lead I broke off into those soft balata covers. All I can say is there was no mistaking those markings on Dad's golf balls—they stood out like pimples on a teenager's nose. I am not sure how counter-productive my excessiveness was, but Dad's brand-new golf balls had slight pieces of lead sticking out of them.

Dad never demeaned my efforts as he gracefully searched in his bag for balls that were not terminally damaged to use in the competition. He politely asked me to give the forever scarred golf balls to his adoring fans in the gallery. Everyone was happy—and, at the time, I didn't know any differently.

I still remember the 17th at the Royal Birkdale Golf Club when I first caddied for Dad. At that time Dad played with the Slazenger B51 golf ball. Dad's drive off the tee found the right rough, where the long, thick grass was nearly eighteen inches long. A slight wind of five to ten miles per hour was at Dad's back, and the yardage to the pin was 247 yards. Dad looked at his golf ball, settled in the lower section of the grass, and grabbed his 7-iron. I was sure he planned to lay up and asked him about his line—I thought he wanted to land the ball in front of the cross bunkers near the green.

Surprised, Dad looked at me and said, "I am putting this on the green."

Dad's powerful swing tore a four- or five-foot strip of grass from the ground. Anyone who has hit from high roughs understands how quickly that grass will grab the club's shaft, turn the clubhead, and result in a quick shot to the left. Not only did Dad keep that 7-iron square, he made great contact with the golf ball. It sailed high and true toward the target. In fact, Dad hit it too strongly. The ball landed on the green, near middle, and bounded over. The ball traveled 265 yards!

I also remember, like it was yesterday, the interview Dad did with ABC sportscaster Dave Marr behind the 18th green following Dad's final round at that Open Championship. I had watched many of Dad's interviews, either from afar on the course or on television at home when I was young. But I had never been a participant in a television interview with Dad. Those cameras were *so big* (really *big*), the stationary setup lights so bright, and the ABC tower so high. I was absolutely scared to death, more a frightened fourteen-year-old than a caddie, as I stood next to Dad in front of those cameras with Dave Marr.

Dave was one of the greats too. He was always kind to me when I traveled with Dad to his tournaments as a kid. Dave was a professional golfer, best known for winning the 1965 PGA

Championship, where he beat Dad and Billy Casper by two strokes for his first and only major championship. Dave was a golf analyst from 1972 to 1991, usually teamed with host Jim McKay. Dave, who passed away in 1997 from stomach cancer, was a great friend of our family too. As Dave conducted the interview, I was so proud of Dad and so proud to be there next to him.

And in those cool moments when the past connects with the present, Dave's son—Dave Marr III—interviewed me and my son Jack III during the 2005 Open Championship at the Old Course at St. Andrews, Scotland, as my dad made his final appearance in that major. At age sixty-five, Dad missed the cut by two strokes, finishing 3 over par at 75–72—147. That year Tiger Woods led wire-to-wire for his tenth major title.

Dave Marr III worked for the Golf Channel at the time, and it was neat to stand with my son Jack III (twenty-nine years later), for such a special interview. That was also the trip where I allowed Jackie, who was fifteen years old at the time (yes, he was underage, and it was illegal) , to have his first beer in one of the local taverns.

One final memory from that 1976 Open Championship—when I first caddied for Dad—is the kind that only a kid's mind can store over the decades.

The summer of 1976 in England was notorious for the extreme heat, lack of rain, and destructive fires. It was the second hottest summer ever in the UK, with an average temperature of 96.6 degrees. At the Open Championship that summer, Mom and I stepped into the elevator at the hotel. An older man stood quietly in the back left corner of the elevator. It was a confined space for three persons. He was easy to notice since, despite the hot summer, he was wearing a full wool suit.

Almost instantly a horrible odor overcame Mom and me—it smelled like fish and chips coated in way too much vinegar. I looked at Mom as I pulled my shirt over my nose and mouth—and began to throw up. I asked her between gags what the horrible smell was. Mom giggled and said, "Zip it." I had to get off the elevator ASAP and began pushing buttons on the panel. When the door opened, I grabbed Mom's hand, and we exited as quickly as possible. Mom giggled again and explained to me the smell was body odor and that the older man most likely had not bathed in quite some time. While the elevator ride was memorable, as I look back, the '76 Open made such an impression on me because I was still so young—caddying at a major for the greatest golfer to ever play the game.

Most fans don't realize that a caddie for one of the top golfers in the world might have to be something of a bodyguard. When I picked up my dad's bag and caddied for him for the first time, I certainly never thought about this aspect of the job.

Safety on the course is always discussed among golfers, caddies, PGA Tour security, and law enforcement. Not that anyone was ever in imminent danger in retrospect, but Dad received death threats while at tournaments. One came before the 1973 Open at Royal Troon, where Dad had special protection for the entire week in his hotel room. Some nut said he wanted to kill Dad and then himself so he would be remembered as a martyr. Another incident came the next year in Los Angeles, around the time when Patty Hearst was kidnapped by the left-wing Symbionese Liberation Army. A policeman who escorted Dad to his room at the Hotel Bel-Air gave him a gun for his protection. Dad didn't feel comfortable or safe in his room, so he left in the middle of the night and walked to a nearby Holiday Inn for a room, where he locked himself in.

At the 1969 PGA Championship at the NCR Country Club, outside Dayton, Ohio, anti-apartheid protestors disrupted play and made it difficult for South African Gary Player. I remember holding Mom's hand as we walked the course watching Dad. We were surrounded by police for protection at all times. Dad and Gary were paired together during one of the rounds when a man, about six-foot-four and 250 pounds, charged the green toward them. Dad was the target. Dad raised his putter in the air and intended to hit the man with it in self-defense, but police officers tackled the man just in time.

Thankfully, no caddie ever had to rush to protect my dad. And Dad's steadfast support of caddies is well known. He didn't rely on one specific caddie during his professional career, though Angelo Argea, Willie Peterson, and Jimmy Dickinson were on his bag many times and were part of his championships.

Angelo, who was known as the "Silver Greek" for his gray afro and who passed away in 2005, was on Dad's bag for forty-four of his seventy PGA Tour wins. In fact, Dad won five of the first six tournaments he played with Angelo on his bag. Willie, who died in 1991, first caddied at the Masters at the age of sixteen and was on Dad's bag for five of his six Masters titles (I was on the bag for Dad's sixth and final Masters win in 1986).

Dad was also inducted into the Caddie Hall of Fame in 1999 (Angelo and Willie are members too). Dad's biographical note for the organization explained:

If it weren't for the experience he gained caddying for his father Charlie at Scioto Country Club near Columbus, Ohio, the man many consider to be the greatest golfer to ever live might never have picked up a club. Jack Nicklaus, winner of a record 18 major championships and 73 PGA TOUR events, began his life in golf as a caddie for his father and has never ceased promoting the important role caddies play in the game.

Whether through his relationships with high-profile caddies, such as Angelo Argea, Willie Peterson and Jimmy Dickinson, or having his sons carry his bag in several major championships, Nicklaus has shown himself to be a steadfast supporter of caddies. For these reasons, he was honored with induction into the Caddie Hall of Fame, which honors those who support caddies and their role in the game of golf.

"I started as a caddie, just like a lot of other kids," Nicklaus said. "If my father hadn't taken me out and said, 'I need somebody to carry the bag,' I wouldn't be here, I'm sure of that."[1]

Dad has never been "clubbed" by a caddie—that is, a caddie never told Dad which club to use or handed him a club for hitting a shot. Dad selected the club himself. For instance, if Dad's approach shot from the fairway was 158 yards to the pin, he might have played six or seven different clubs. He might have choked down on a 4-iron or hit a 9-iron to spin the ball.

The longer I caddied for Dad, the more I realized my main responsibility was to be his friend on the course. Yes, I did the tasks required as his caddie. I cleaned his clubs, held the umbrella when it rained, marked his golf balls, tended the pin, helped him sidestep any distractions. But my job was to be his friend and, if necessary, help him refocus.

Here's an example: I was on Dad's bag at Augusta, and he had a 155-yard shot over a front bunker to the pin. When Dad rolled the sod over his 7-iron and the ball landed in the bunker, he said, "I think there's something wrong with that ball." I asked him what he meant, and Dad said he felt the ball's flight wasn't correct. But I knew he hit the ball fat (where the club face penetrates the ground before it makes contact with the ball) because I heard the sound.

I said, "Dad, you hit the shot fat."

Dad's immediate answer was, "No, I didn't."

I quickly learned my response wasn't what Dad needed to hear. Dad controlled what he could control on the course, and, in his mind, the ball didn't fly like it should. I learned after a short time as Dad's caddie to be more supportive and act as his friend. It was a quick learning experience as I took that golf ball out of play before the next hole.

After Dad won the '86 Masters, Greg Norman, who finished tied for second with Tom Kite, thought having me on the bag was the secret sauce to his win. I regret to say I was not the secret sauce. It just so happened that Dad was a great player, and he dragged me along on that victory.

I have been very blessed to play a lot of golf with my dad and to caddie for him. I have watched him compete, I have watched him win, I have watched him get beat, and I have watched him build his incredible legacy. I learned more caddying for Dad than I ever did playing the game of golf. As his caddie, I also learned about golf course management, game management, and, frankly, life management.

But it all comes back to that first time I caddied for Dad at the Open Championship. It wasn't my goal to be his caddie. It just happened. I had to grow up quickly in so many ways, and it couldn't have been a better experience as I learned so many life lessons.

CHAPTER 16

Focus More on Your Family Than on Work

The stories and statistics I've shared throughout this book have made it clear that Dad was a busy guy. His travel was extensive and exhausting. The demands for his attention—between on-course play, off-course obligations like media interviews, and several business relationships—required that he be laser-focused on whatever he was doing at that moment.

But one thing he determined early was to find ways he could do things with his children, where his attention was undivided. One of those places was out in the wild, and from my earliest memories, some of our closest moments and best family stories occurred where the nearest phone lines might be hundreds of miles away.

Dad has always been a huge outdoorsman. He loves to hunt and fish. One reason Dad said he moved from his hometown of Columbus to North Palm Beach in 1967 was because the fishing was so good.

While all of us children grew to share his passion, I promise you, what we really enjoyed on those trips was the total attention that came with them. There were no interruptions, no phones, and no distractions. We had Dad's full attention.

Thinking back on all those trips, I almost feel inept as a father because Dad did so many great things with me when I was young. Dad has established a very high bar as a father by which I often measure myself. I am forever grateful for my times with Dad. Although my family may not go on as many trips, I so treasure the times I share with my children.

Dad to this day still loves to take the family—specifically the four boys—on hunting and fishing trips. When his schedule allows him a breather, he can usually be found with a fishing pole in his hand.

One of my favorite photographs of Dad and me was taken when I was a young child, maybe five or six years old. It's a small black-and-white photo of me falling back into Dad's arms after I fired a shotgun for the first time. The photo serves as a reminder that there are opportunities when it doesn't cost a penny to spend time with your kids. At the time, we still lived in Columbus, and I tagged along with Dad and my Grandpa Charlie on a duck hunt. I was in a muddy field playing with the spent shells that ejected from their shotguns when they fired at the ducks overhead. The mud and shells were the perfect combo—I didn't care about the ducks.

When Dad was finished, he asked me if I wanted to shoot his shotgun. He stooped behind me and positioned the gun against my right shoulder. When I pulled the trigger, the force of the blast knocked me backward into Dad's arms. That cool moment was caught forever as my grandfather snapped a photo of us, and that picture hung on my wall for years.

Though I loved the time with Dad, I would grow to have mixed emotions about big game hunting when I was young.

I was fourteen years old and had never killed any four-legged animal. I had shot turkeys and ducks but never a deer. In 1976 Dad went out with a few of his buddies to hunt elk in Vermejo, New Mexico, for eight days. He telephoned home and asked my brother Steve and me to join him for the last few days.

I had never handled a big gun before, so when we arrived that night, Dad took Steve and me to shoot at a few practice targets. The next morning, we drove by Jeep to where we planned to hunt. The guide explained we had to walk from that point, and we started up over a hill. Just as we reached the summit, there stood a huge royal elk on an opposite hill, about 150 yards away.

The elk had been injured somehow, in a fight or something, because he wasn't strong enough to run straight up the hill. He began running across the slope. The guide said, "He's a beauty; if you can get a shot, take it." Even before Steve could get a shell in the chamber, I fired an offhanded shot at the elk and hit it in the neck. I just aimed for his head and neck and pulled the trigger. The elk tumbled over on its back, dead. The elation of having hit the elk was quickly followed by a strange disillusionment. I was like, "Wow, is that what big game hunting is about?" We never got to what was the official start of the hunt because I had shot the elk on our way to the site we had selected. It was over before it started. And as accurate as the gun was, there was no real challenge in it.

The following year Dad took Steve and me to Brooks Range in northern Alaska to fish and hunt Dall sheep, a wild sheep native to northwestern North America. The average height and weight of an adult Dall sheep is 4.6 feet and 150 pounds. We caught a few Arctic char, closely related to both salmon and lake trout, and that part of the trip was fantastic. We saw a few bears, and that was amazing too.

The next day we flew in a Piper Super Cub—a backcountry airplane—into the wilderness and landed on the Arctic tundra. We hiked for seven days and slept in tents that we carried in our hunting backpacks. The nighttime conversations around the campsite were so much fun, and we talked about everything and made fun of each other. Both Dad and Steve each shot and killed a Dall sheep. There were two days left in the hunt, and I had been reluctant to shoot because of my experience the previous year with the royal elk. Then one of the prized sheep ended up just a hundred yards in front of me. Dad encouraged me to take at least one shot, saying, "You've come all the way to Alaska. There's a beautiful Dall sheep right there. You need to shoot it."

I took the shot, hit it, and the Dall sheep dropped dead. When I lifted its head, air rushed out of its mouth in a deep gasp. It scared the heck out of me.

That was it, I told myself. I knew that Dad was bringing us on these trips because we were getting time and making memories with him, but I couldn't big-game hunt again. Spending time with Dad and Steve was always special. But, suddenly, a rifle hunt was about killing two beautiful animals. That made me uneasy. Honestly, I didn't want to go. And I didn't go on another big-game hunt until my senior year in college.

During that window of time, I was actively chasing my hopes of becoming better at golf. Dad understood my hesitancy about going on the hunting trips, so he made it a point to get me my one-on-one time out on the course. Again, what makes Dad so special is that he knew how I struggled with the hunting trips that gave him joy. Rather than ignoring my situation, he quietly looked for a different opportunity to give me that "me" time.

A few years later Dad bought me a Golden Eagle Archery bow while I was in college. It was an antiquated compound bow, and Dad said I might want to try it on a hunt. It was a subtle way for him to try to get me back out in the wild with him and my brothers. I practiced and practiced with it, and after several months of work, Dad took Steve, Gary, and me to Montana. I loved every minute of the trip even though I never once shot an arrow.

Over the next twelve years we went on hunts, and I never let loose an arrow. I promise you that each of those years we worked our fannies off, hiking up and down the hills. One year we were at Flathead Lake, a large natural lake in northwest Montana, south of Kalispell. From there we hiked into the wilderness areas. We saw this big bull elk that made a shrill rutting call known as bugling. We bugled back, and the bugles went back and forth. We even had it in our sights a few times. Still, I never actually let loose an arrow.

That's when I fell in love with hunting again—without ever taking a shot. Hunting was not about killing an animal anymore. It was about spending time with Dad and my brothers. I didn't recognize that when I was fourteen. But as I have gotten older, I have learned how to cherish those moments. We didn't kill an animal on that hunt, and I couldn't wait to go hunting again with Dad and my brothers. As a family, we have had some of the best experiences and times while hunting and fishing with Dad. Even to this day we usually try to hunt as a family once a year.

While it's not about killing an animal, I am not opposed to hunting, and over the years I have taken down animals. I had to go through a mental process to fall in love with hunting again—but now I love to hunt. I think back to that time in Montana as we chased that big bull elk. Dad was hiking that mountain with us, sweating his butt off, working hard, and having fun. Dad is very competitive in everything he does. He wanted to get an elk with a bow as badly as any of us. But it was more about the journey, about the challenge. And it was a challenge. It became more of a challenge each year when we didn't achieve our ultimate goal of tagging our elk.

Sometimes Dad was able to both find something we as kids wanted to do and also teach a lesson at the same time. I remember Christmas morning when I was fourteen. Steve and Dad had identical gifts underneath the Christmas tree at our home in North Palm Beach. Each gift had the same colored bow and wrapping paper. Dad said, "Steve, let's open these boxes together." Inside were boxing gloves. The rest of the family all looked at each other, confused.

Steve had pushed the envelope at home for several months, getting a little pushy and even a little physical with the rest of us.

As he and Dad unwrapped their boxing gloves, Dad said, "Steve, I like that you want to box a little recently, and today we are going to see who's the boss of this household, who's the big guy, who is going to make the decisions for the family. And we're going to settle it right now."

Steve's eyes got big, but he had been egging this on.

They proceeded to put on their boxing gloves. Dad told the rest of us to stay inside while they went outside to the backyard. We watched through the kitchen window as Dad walked toward Steve. Dad lightly peppered Steve on the chest, the shoulder, the chin. They weren't hard pops, and we heard Dad say, "So you think you're the big guy, you can make the decisions in this house. Well, come on. Let's see who's the big guy here." We all prayed Steve wouldn't take a swing at Dad. Thankfully, Steve just backpedaled, and it lasted only a few minutes. Dad didn't have any intention to hurt Steve, but he wanted to get his point across—and he did it by giving Steve a gift he had thought he wanted.

Dad had his arm around Steve's shoulders when they walked back in the house. Steve had tears in his eyes, but there was a new respect and warmth that all of us could see.

A lesson taught as only Dad could.

While the boys went on hunting and fishing trips, Dad made it a point to also have a special time for our sister, Nan. Dad has always bought Nan an antique for her birthday and Christmas. She has the most wonderful collection of antiques from around the world, saying the annual gesture is a special bond between her and Dad. Dad also took Nan to the Open in Europe when he competed. They had visited different countries in Europe leading up to the tournament. One time Nan bugged Dad about how much she wanted to go to Paris. He said, "Yeah, yeah, yeah," acting as if he was ignoring her. But Dad surprised Nan with dinner in Paris.

Dad always teases Nan that she is his favorite daughter; Nan teases him and says he's her favorite dad.

Like each of the boys and our various trips into the wild, Nan's trophy was spending time with Dad. That carried far greater value than collected antiques or meals in Paris.

Whether Dad was with us on a golf course or in the middle of a cold stream catching fish, it didn't matter what we did that day—we always ended up together at the dinner table that evening. In fact, Mom and Dad have had the same wooden dinner table for the past fifty years in their North Palm Beach home. It is the table where I sat as a child with the family as Mom, Dad, and my siblings shared stories of whatever was on our minds. Mom and Dad have also shared that table with the outside world. Magic Chef, an appliance brand, once shot a commercial of Mom in front of her radar range oven, and Dad did a commercial shoot at the table for one of the first mobile phones—it was as large as a breadbasket! I have grown and learned to appreciate the time we have spent together around that same table, which now also includes my children, nephews, and nieces.

It also gives us time to reflect and embrace the great big world we live in.

Dad always called family the "crux of everything" he did in golf and in business. He certainly proved that time and time again during his years on the tour. Earlier, I touched on Dad's commitment to never spend more than two weeks on the road at a time. He went out of his way to return home as much as he could. No matter where in the world he was and how far he had to travel, Dad always found a way to put family first. Over the years, after I had become a father myself, I increasingly realized how important it was to spend time with my children—and the sacrifices Dad made to be with us as much as he could.

The PGA Tour asked Dad about why he went out of his way to spend time at home, and he offered a surprising answer: "My family was more important than my golf game," he said. "I became a better golfer."[1]

Mom also talked to the PGA about how Dad would always find a way to be there for us, including at our games. "I think our children at the time thought, 'Well, that's just what dads do,'" Mom told the PGA. "Of course now that they're married and have families of their own, they'll say to me sometimes, 'Wow, I had no idea what Dad gave up to watch us.' . . . It makes them even more proud of their dad."[2]

Even when he was the best golfer on the planet, Dad focused more on his family than work. His time at home and with us kids grounded him. Those moments reminded him of what was truly important and helped recharge him.

All of us have busy lives as we deal with the pressures of being a parent, trying to provide for our families, and being successful at work. We should never put work before our families, especially our children. Even with our busy schedules, we need to carve out time for them—in doing so, perhaps we'll find our purpose renewed. After all, putting family first helped make my dad the greatest golfer of all time.

CHAPTER 17

Be Charitable and Don't Draw Attention to Yourself

It was Mom's vision, but it changed Dad's life toward the end of his playing career.

It is true that golf has a long-standing history of raising money for charities. In January 2020 the PGA Tour announced its tournaments had surpassed $3 billion in charity giving, supporting causes from pediatric cancer research to Special Olympics to military veterans.

Independently, many other golfers—including Dad and Mom—have become major forces in charitable fundraising.

When Dad was playing, he said he was tangentially aware of the importance of raising money for charities. He played in a ton of exhibitions over the years, many of them for charitable causes. Some of his favorite events back in the day were with iconic comedian and actor Bob Hope. (One of my adult sons Googled Bob Hope because he didn't recognize the name!) Helping raise donations for charity was what Dad and all golfers did, but it wasn't at the front of his mind. Winning was.

Then Mom took charge.

Mom has always been extremely passionate about giving back—specifically by bringing health care to as many children as possible. And today Mom and Dad are building a legacy of charity with the Nicklaus Children's Health Care Foundation at its core. They started the foundation in 2004, and since then it has raised more than $100 million.

The ability to change lives has brought Mom and Dad incredible joy and fulfillment. Dad absolutely loves interacting with the kids. In fact, Mom joked that Dad's commitment to the foundation has forced her to add another zero to the oversize check she presents him at the end of each fundraising year—from zero, to double zero, to triple zero, and so on! Dad is constantly on the prowl for items others might value that he can bring in to the fundraising efforts, from memorabilia to trips to speeches to experiences with his peers. He even took one item off his own wrist when he auctioned off an eighteen-karat gold Rolex watch he had owned for fifty years to benefit the foundation. The winning bid was $1.2 million!

Dad has said when he first started working on behalf of the charity it was difficult to ask for $1,000. But the closer he is drawn to the children and their families, the easier the ask has become. Today he doesn't bat an eye when asking someone to make a $1 million contribution.

When it comes to children's diseases, many of the most impactful stories never have a chance to be heard. Mom and Dad work to highlight the stories that are close to their hearts.

Mention the names of five-year-old twins Teegan and Riley and watch Dad's blue eyes light up. Riley was healthy at birth, but Teegan was born with one lung and half of a heart that was positioned backward in her chest. Doctors at the Minnesota hospital where the twins were born told the family that Teegan's condition was inoperable and that they didn't expect her to live long. They sent Teegan home and encouraged the family to enjoy their short time together with the twins. Ten weeks later, however, Teegan was still fighting to live. Her mother, desperate to help her daughter, researched multiple pediatric hospitals around the country and telephoned each one.

The only call that was returned was from surgeon Redmond Burke, whom Mom and Dad call one of their "angel doctors" at Nicklaus Children's Hospital in Miami. Dr. Burke told Teegan's mom, "The word *inoperable* is not in my vocabulary." He went to work and over the next six months performed six operations to rebuild her heart. During that period, both Mom and Dad heard Teegan's story and started visiting her, thinking they would encourage her. It didn't take long for the roles to reverse. Teegan became such an inspiration to them that Dad said, "Helping a child is far more important than making any four-foot putt."

So sure was Dr. Burke of the medical success that he ultimately told Teegan's mom to take her home to live and grow up with her twin sister, Riley. Teegan was enrolled in kindergarten in the fall of 2020 and, according to her mother, was doing well. When a healing garden was dedicated at the Nicklaus Children's Hospital in Miami—it's located in an outdoor courtyard and provides hospitalized patients and families a quiet space—Teegan and Riley released butterflies in celebration.

There is also a young child from Venezuela who came to the

Nicklaus Children's Hospital in Miami and displayed remarkable courage. She wore a beautiful low-cut dress to show off the big scar on her chest that she refers to as her "badge of life" following a scary operation. When she spoke at the Nicklaus Children's Hospital annual gala, she spoke with such confidence. She has a wonderful spirit.

In 2015, when Mom and Dad proposed a $60 million gift to Miami Children's Health Systems, the hospital's leaders also asked if they could change the hospital's name to the Nicklaus Children's Hospital. The hospital leadership felt the Nicklaus name and brand would extend its reach well beyond Coral Gables.

Once a small charity aimed at serving children in Palm Beach County, the Nicklaus Children's Health Care Foundation has grown into an international organization. It focuses on the diagnosis, treatment, and prevention of childhood illnesses and provides programs and services free of charge to more than four thousand hospitalized children like Teegan and their families. By the year 2020, the rapidly growing network of facilities supported by the foundation included the following:

- Nicklaus Children's Hospital Outpatient Center at Legacy Place in Palm Beach Gardens;
- Nicklaus Children's Hospital (Miami);
- Jupiter Medical Center, which opened the De George Pediatric Unit with Nicklaus Children's Hospital;
- the Advanced Pediatric Care Pavilion (APC) at Nicklaus Children's Hospital;

- Nicklaus Children's Health System, including Nicklaus Children's Hospital Foundation;
- Nicklaus Children's Health Care Foundation of Canada; and
- the Fetal Care Center at Nicklaus Children's Hospital.

Mom and Dad have good reasons—ones that hit close to home—to focus their charitable efforts on children.

In 1966, when our sister, Nan, was not quite a year old, she experienced choking issues. It was the strangest thing and had doctors baffled because there would be periods where she would choke and be unable to breathe, but a few minutes later she would be just fine. There were times when Mom yelled for Dad, who might have been in another room. By the time Dad reached them, Nan would be fine. After two months of doctors' appointments, Mom and Dad took Nan to the Nationwide Children's Hospital in Columbus. An X-ray showed a shadow. Then a bronchoscope showed that she had inhaled a crayon, and pieces of it were lodged in her windpipe. When the pieces moved, they made Nan choke. Nan underwent a procedure to remove the crayon pieces, but during the surgery, a piece made its way into her lung, and she was forced to spend six days in an oxygen tent. Mom and Dad were uncertain if Nan would survive, but, thankfully, we had a happy ending.

Mom has often shared with us that while sitting with Nan, she and Dad agreed that if they ever were in a position to make a difference in their world, they would focus on children's health care and those who provide it. It took a few years, but they are quickly making up for that time with all they are doing today.

A second incident deepened their commitment further. In 2005 Mom and Dad established "The Jake" pro-am golf tournament at The Bear's Club in Jupiter, Florida. The two-day event is held in memory of their grandson and my nephew Jake Nicklaus. Jake, the seventeen-month-old son of my younger brother Steve and his wife, Krista, drowned in a hot tub in 2005. "The Jake" annually brings in millions of dollars and has become the foundation's chief fundraiser.

Mom and Dad hold several signature and beneficiary fundraising events each year. The Fore Love Tournament is a tennis-golf tournament that they cohost with the winningest doubles tennis team ever, Mike and Bob Bryan. They are also involved in the annual Honda Classic PGA Tour event in Palm Beach. The Golden Heart Luncheon is cochaired by Mom along with my sister, Nan O'Leary, and my wife, Alli. The luncheon's former guest speakers include First Lady Laura Bush, entertainer Marie Osmond, and actress Katherine Heigl.

At the 2020 Golden Heart Luncheon, which attracted almost four hundred attendees and raised $550,000, keynote speaker, actress, and philanthropist Jane Seymour said Mom and Dad "understand that what you leave behind is the love you shared in life and the difference you've made."[1]

Even the story behind Dad's habit of wearing a yellow shirt or a yellow sweater on Sundays (usually the day featuring the final round of tournaments) has a charitable component. Dad wore that color in honor of Craig Smith, the son of Mom's minister when Dad and Mom lived in Ohio. Craig was diagnosed with bone cancer (Ewing's sarcoma) at age eleven and died at thirteen in 1971.

Before he passed, Craig received a promise from Dad—that Dad would start wearing a yellow shirt in the final rounds of tournaments as a way of showing he was thinking of Craig. Dad often telephoned him and sent souvenirs from tournaments. But, more important, Dad kept his promise to wear yellow on Sundays.

It worked in the 1986 Masters. Dad hadn't won a tournament in two years, a major in six years, and a Masters since 1975. But then on Sunday of the '86 Masters, he pulled a yellow shirt over his head and won the tournament. In 2019, in partnership with the PGA Tour and the Children's Miracle Network, Mom and the foundation launched a "Play Yellow" campaign to raise money for children's hospitals and as a way to honor Craig. Their initiative is to raise $100 million for children's hospitals over the next five years.

Today the Nicklaus name carries significant weight in the charity world, which has opened opportunities for me and my children to get involved with exceptional efforts and causes. Since 2018 I have been a board member for WorldServe International, which is based in Branson, Missouri. Founded in 1996, the organization is dedicated to becoming a leading provider of clean water wells for the 319 million people in sub-Saharan Africa. Women and children there spend up to six hours each day walking miles to collect water that is contaminated and unsafe and leads to all kinds of illnesses and infections. The organization raises funds that go toward building sustainable, solar-operated, deep-borehole wells in villages. The cost for each well is between $45,000 and $50,000, and the organization has built more than 2,500 wells.

In Tanzania, for example, twenty-five million people still lack access to clean water. Women and children walk an average of 3.7 miles per day to collect unfit water. The goal in 2020—prior to the coronavirus pandemic—was to build fourteen solar-powered water projects at a total investment of $700,000.

In 2018 Dad and I traveled to Tanzania along with WorldServe International President and CEO John Bongiorno and my former high school football coach Tom Mullins, the founder and former pastor at Christ Fellowship Church in Palm Beach. There were two main reasons for the trip: we dedicated a new water well and shared the message of Christ with villagers. We were also joined by professional basketball player Malcolm Brogdon of the Milwaukee Bucks, who launched his organization Hoops2o in 2018, which also raises funds to build water wells in East Africa. Malcom's organization was built under the umbrella of the Waterboys, an initiative started by then–Philadelphia Eagles defensive end Chris Long (who retired from the NFL in 2019) to provide clean, accessible drinking water to people worldwide.

There's plenty of water in Africa, but it's mostly underground, and there are plenty of problems getting to it. The social upheaval is alarming. Many children don't go to school because they spend most of their day walking miles to collect water. Women are also raped during their daylong trips to collect water. As one might imagine, it is incredible to see the beautiful smiles on the faces of the people when their village has an operational water well. They turn a faucet and clean water fills a large container. It's a fairly simple process. Wells are typically six hundred feet deep, and the power to the pump is generated by a solar panel.

My wife, Alli, is actively engaged in fundraising. She brings great energies and a caring heart to all children and their health care needs. She is always the first to raise a hand when help is required. One charity she has embraced is the Center for Family Services of Palm Beach County, Inc. Since 1961 the organization has been serving families and children in Palm Beach County through an array of services to help them get back on their feet.

The power of charity has extended to my five children as well. It's an extension of what Mom and Dad taught me about the responsibility to give back.

One of our family commitments is to donate the funds (around $50,000) to build a water well—probably in Tanzania—through WorldServe International. My children are 100 percent on board to help make this happen, and I was fortunate enough to take four of my children with me to Tanzania for the first time a few years ago. My daughter Casey, who lives in New York and has always been our caregiver, fell in love with what is happening there. To watch my kids interact with the villagers' children was heartwarming. We brought them toys and coloring books, and it was neat to experience. During another trip to the Congo-Rwanda border, we met a young man named Frederick, who had both of his arms chopped off during the country's military conflict. Yet he paints with the nubs of his arms and operates a school there for children.

My children are also involved in the Nicklaus Children's Health Care Foundation as well as the Nicklaus Children's Hospital in Miami. They have worked as hosts for fundraisers associated with the facilities in addition to events during the annual Memorial Tournament.

But I don't want them to experience just the fundraising efforts. I also want them to get involved in the purpose of what we are doing. It's an emotional experience when you walk through the neonatal intensive care unit. Some of these infants are the size of the palm of your hand. And the work we are trying to do provides the highest level of care for thousands of babies each year. When my children see the benefits of all the work their parents and grandparents are trying to do, the whole experience becomes more impactful and personal for them.

I don't have to ask them to get involved. They can't wait for the next opportunity.

CHAPTER 18

See the Bigger Picture

I didn't fully appreciate Dad's ability to see the bigger picture in nearly everything he did until I became a partner in his company Nicklaus Design. It's unbelievable that he still has the energy and imagination for golf course design and management at his age. Dad is the point person on projects from start to finish, and he has an innate ability to see a pasture and turn it into an unforgettable experience.

Even though Dad has turned eighty-one, he hasn't shown any signs of slowing down. He has traveled incessantly over the years, and the Golden Bear brand has a global reach. The business includes golf course design, the development of golf and real estate communities, and the marketing and licensing of lifestyle products. The company sells items such as golf balls, art, wine, lemonade, sunscreen, lip balm, and shampoos. The breadth of Dad's activities led his fellow golfer Chi-Chi Rodríguez to teasingly call him a "legend in his spare time."

While Dad is proud of his lip balm, he feels the most comfortable in a golf cart with a pencil and notepad in his hand, scratching out a new hole. The course design business remains Dad's passion. Over the years Nicklaus Design has created nearly 450 courses worldwide that are open for play in forty-five countries and forty states in the United States.

There are two things required to create a business such as the one that has developed all of those golf courses. One is a great name; the other is a great vision. Throughout this book we have focused on how diligently Dad lived to protect his name. From imagining shots in his mind to raising his family, Dad also brought a vision to everything he did. His capacity to stand on a green and, in his mind, immediately lift himself to thirty thousand feet to see the entire course is unnatural. His ability to find new perspectives and move his ideas out of his imagination into reality can be seen not only in raising his children but also in his work as a golf course designer. Over the years, in the conversations we've had about both business and life, Dad has encouraged me not to get caught in the weeds. Too many businessmen—and fathers—become so focused on moments that are irrelevant in the grand scheme of things that they miss the opportunity to appreciate a greater picture.

With my own children, I often had to remember that the mistakes they made weren't reflective of who they were as people. Instead, I had to see them as moments for growth. But keeping that perspective is difficult. We have to see a project—or a family—for what it really is instead of getting mired in the minutiae.

But for all the times Dad told me not to get tripped up in the small things, it was not until we built a golf course together that I learned what he really meant. As he explained how all that I was learning could make me a better father, those words made even more sense.

Dad was nudged into the golf course design business in 1965 by a fledging course designer named Pete Dye. Pete designed more than one hundred courses over his career before his death in 2020 at ninety-four, and back then he asked Dad to look over what would become the Golf Club near Columbus with him. Dad knew his hometown area firsthand and made a few suggestions that Dye liked and incorporated into his design of the course.

Two years later Charles Fraser, at Sea Pines Resort in South Carolina, was looking to do a project called Harbour Town Golf Links. Charles called Mark McCormack, the founder of IMG and Dad's agent. Mark recommended Dad because of his interest in golf course design. Dad quickly told Charles that his interest in design did not mean he knew how to actually do it, but he knew a person who did—Pete Dye. Although Charles had never heard of Pete, he hired him, while Dad stayed on as Pete's consultant. The pair designed the acclaimed Harbour Town Golf Links in Hilton Head, which still hosts the RBC Heritage PGA Tour event and challenges golfers to rely on finesse and shot-making rather than strength.

Dad may have stayed on longer as Pete's consultant but said he couldn't afford to do so. Dad made twenty-three trips to Harbour Town yet was never reimbursed for his travel because Pete put any earnings back into the half-dozen golf courses he did with Dad from 1969 to 1971. So Dad finally said, "Pete, I love working with you. But I can't afford to be your partner!"

By that time Dad had established himself as one of the world's best golfers, and his interest in golf course design as a secondary career was growing. In 1972 Dad started to raise the money that he needed to build Muirfield Village Golf Club in Dublin, Ohio, outside of Columbus. Dad teamed with Desmond Muirhead, a well-known golf course designer, on the project. It is the only golf course in the world to host the Ryder Cup, Solheim Cup, and Presidents Cup. It also was the site of the 1992 U.S. Amateur.

Ed Etchells, the first course superintendent at Muirfield Village, noted that Dad's design style didn't include many blueprints, saying, "Mostly it was Jack's verbal instruction and waving his arms."[1] Dad's design blended in elevated vantage points—often called stadium golf—to give spectators a better view.

The course wasn't even complete when the business side of running a club became a focus. With his ability to see the bigger picture, Dad has shared that he always disliked courses that discriminated when creating a leadership team. So from the very beginning, he made sure the club's board was racial and gender inclusive.

As I look back, Dad's vision and execution amaze me. He was barely thirty years old when he began his dream of Muirfield Village, which remains a standard for all courses.

Dad and Desmond, who died in 2002 at seventy-nine, teamed up on another half-dozen golf courses before Dad ventured out on his own. The first course Dad designed by himself was Glen Abbey Golf Club, outside of Toronto, in 1976. The course was home to the Canadian Open for thirty years.

Dad's efforts to always see the bigger picture included making sure that in every transaction he did what he knew was the right thing, on the golf course and in the boardroom. In life or business, Dad will never negotiate away his integrity. He has always believed a good deal is not one-sided. It must be good for both parties to be successful.

And whether a deal might be tilted in Dad's favor or not, he has relied on an important component he taught me when I joined him in business: always overdeliver. Dad always gives more than what he promised since he believes going above and beyond adds value to the partnership and separates him from his competitors. For instance, Dad might be contracted to visit a new golf site two or three times. However, he routinely visits sites many more times than contracted to make sure his partners are pleased with the direction and progress. Or he might be scheduled to be at a site for a half-day, but he stays the entire day. And when days turn into evenings, he'll have his crew drive their cars and trucks to the site and turn on their headlights so everyone can see the terrain.

Overdelivering applies to other parts of life, Dad often told me. If you tell a person you are going to do something, you must do all that you said—plus some. You can't always do it, but you have to try.

It remains such a privilege to work alongside Dad and share thoughts and ideas on golf design and strategy. I am always amazed by his ability to see things from thirty thousand feet. It's the big picture that is most important to the developer. The golf course is often the centerpiece of a community, but all the components must complement the others with the best use of available space. Dad's participation here clearly adds value. However, some of our best golf courses and surrounding communities are the result of a team approach. Golf course design is truly an exercise in problem solving and managing the talents of the team. Whether we are working a Signature (Dad's premier product), a Legacy (a co-design by Dad and me), or a Nicklaus Design, Dad remains our inspiration and leader. We design to a budget, not budget to a design. Dad has taught me that any project worth doing is worth doing 100 percent, and he always strives to create something very special that is tailored to our clients. I am proud to carry that torch.

Sometimes seeing the bigger picture might require walking away from a deal. Dad has learned over the years that some new owners just want to put together a golf course and get out of town. They might want the Nicklaus brand associated with the course, but they won't utilize our input or expertise. That can only lead to potential issues down the road for everyone.

People have often assumed that being a good golfer makes Dad a better designer. But Dad would counter that seeing the bigger picture makes him a better designer—and a better golfer. He can envision how golfers should play a hole by the way he designed it, and this vision comes through in his designs: Dad's golf courses are ultimately enjoyable to play. They will share certain foundations, such as a solid golf strategy with risk versus reward options. For example, Dad will set up a golf hole with water down the right side on the tee shot and sand bunkering protecting the left side of the green. Therefore, if golfers challenge the water on the tee shot, the green approach opens. Conversely, if golfers bail out away from water on the tee shot, they will have to contend with the bunkers on approach.

Unlike the majority of us, Dad could put the ball exactly where he wanted it. Such ability has allowed Dad to be a great manager of his golf game. Understanding the strategy of each hole and his abilities to perform a certain golf shot remain a good formula for Dad. He knows when to be aggressive, and he knows when to play more conservatively. He says that knowledge helps but points out that golfers must also execute their shots. Not every professional baseball player can hit a curveball even when they know it's coming, right?

Dad once gave a clinic at a new course (not one he designed), where amateurs and pros alike played in the grand opening. The course was beautifully manicured with trees, water, great service, and a spacious clubhouse on a hill. It had it all. After their rounds, the amateurs mostly commented that it was maybe the most beautiful course they had ever played. In contrast, the pros were very disappointed in the golf course. The pros were more focused on shot values.

What did that mean to Dad?

The average golfer probably doesn't care or doesn't really know what a good golf course is. They are interested in something that's well conditioned, something that's pretty, something to have fun with their friends playing, and everyone has a good day. The pros talked about how the golf course played, how the first green held a shot, the sight lines. Dad's belief was that the best courses could actually satiate both extremes with enough tough shots to please the pros and enough aesthetic pleasure for the amateurs. Finding that sweet spot to make both groups happy requires seeing the bigger picture.

All of these lessons came together for me when I went to work on my first golf course in 1988, Hanbury Manor Golf Club. As a player I tried to stay in the moment, looking at each hole and each shot as independently important. But now I had to try to rise up like Dad. Even though Dad did not give me specific instructions, my responsibility was to create an 18-hole experience.

Following my dad's lessons, I continued to design golf courses—and found my passion. In a neat design trifecta, Dad, my brother Steve, and I each designed a course at the Club at Ibis in Palm Beach Gardens. In fact, Ibis is the first country club community with three Nicklaus-designed courses—the Legend, designed by Dad; the Tradition, designed by Steve; and the Heritage, designed by me.

In March 2020 I was promoted to vice chairman of the Nicklaus Companies, allowing me more opportunities to learn from and work alongside my dad. I have been responsible for the design of more than thirty-five golf courses worldwide, including sixteen co-designs with Dad.

I've tried to channel all that I've learned from golf into different aspects of my life. Golf, sports, and business can teach you many important lessons in life that can be applied to any obstacle. It's about preparation, execution, and treating people fairly. Dad has always been kindhearted and had a human approach.

I grew up with the best teacher in the world in Dad.

He showed me how to take a simple idea like the game of golf and break down the lessons it teaches you. In life, like golf, we are not always playing from the middle of the fairway. There will be rough patches. Often we learn more about ourselves when faced with this adversity. If presented a challenge, do we take a mighty swing and accept any potential risks, or do we chip out and start over? It is my opinion that if we take a step back from any situation, we might see the bigger picture. Dad has always been able to do just that and live his life with clarity and purpose.

Continuing to see the bigger picture, Dad wants to help identify and create the next great frontiers for golf. One of his most heartfelt projects has been the renovation of a course in Grand Haven, Michigan, located on the eastern shore of Lake Michigan, which was scheduled to open in early 2021. The course will reopen as American Dunes Golf Club, dedicated to the military and the families of fallen service personnel.

All profits from American Dunes will be donated to Folds of Honor, which offers educational scholarships for the spouses and children of disabled veterans and fallen soldiers. Folds of Honor—named for the creases in an American flag after it is removed from the caskets of fallen soldiers—was founded in 2007 by US Air Force Reserves Lieutenant Colonel Dan Rooney, who is also a professional golf instructor. Rooney, who fought in the war in Iraq as an F-16 fighter pilot, has worked alongside Dad on the course.

Dad never served in the military, but he believes so much in the project that he donated his design fee. More notably, Dad has put in the time. As we get older, our time becomes very significant. Dad is committed to American Dunes and its mission by creating something very special. Each hole on the 7,213-yard, par-73 course will honor a fallen solider with his or her story, alongside a plaque commemorating each of Dad's eighteen professional majors. "Taps"—the bugle call played during flag ceremonies and at military services—will be played every day on the course at 1300 hours (1:00 p.m.), and the dining room is designed as a fighting squadron bar.

With his work on Americans Dunes, Dad continues to see the bigger picture. Golf is a great game, but the sacrifices that our military families and veterans make transcend it. Dad and the entire Nicklaus Designs team are proud to have honored our heroes in our own small way.

Sometimes, seeing the bigger picture requires a second look at past projects, using the perspectives you've developed in a lifetime of experiences. Dad has done that recently, overseeing a course renovation at Muirfield. Dad has described the project as his "last bite at the apple" as the entire course is reworked.

If I were to pick one golf course that best embodies my father, it would be Muirfield Village Golf Club. It is his flagship course, in his hometown. It was my dad's dream to create a championship golf course that could host the best players in the world. Muirfield Village Golf Club hosts the Memorial Tournament, which remains a favorite stop for the PGA Tour while raising significant charitable dollars for children's health care. At the same time the Memorial Tournament pays tribute to those who have served the game of golf so well.

Dad took the opportunity to update and modernize the course with today's players and equipment in mind. Dad's first obligation was to make sure the course's new design challenges both professionals and amateurs, including moving the tees back, adjusting bunker locations, and recontouring the greens. The changes are quite subtle, where most return golfers will not notice a difference. In fact, the greens are now more receptive to an approach shot, with larger pinnable areas. Our ability to firm up the greens will be the big factor going forward with the new greens mix. Dad did not set out to make Muirfield tougher; he set out to make Muirfield better—and he has done just that.

What it comes down to is making sure everyone has a great experience. Dad wants people to walk away and say, "Man, that's a great golf course. What time can I play it again tomorrow?"

AFTERWORD

Leave a Legacy That Lasts for Generations

Jack Nicklaus is simply the greatest man I have ever known. He is my role model. He is my best friend. He is my dad.

It has been fun for me to relive a lifetime of experiences and lessons from a father to a son and to share their significance as I raised my family.

As I sat down with my friend Don Yaeger, he explained that he had great confidence in my story. He also suggested that my journey might reveal something I will treasure for the rest of my life. Don was spot-on.

For me, *Best Seat in the House* can begin and end with this treasure: There was one particular afternoon (like so many we shared at Don's home) when I was asked to quickly describe the relationships I share with each of my children. On the surface it was a casual question, and I began with a somewhat casual response—then made a complete *stop*.

Relationships, as we all know, can be complex, involved, and very different.

My mind went blank. I found myself in that moment unable to verbalize the relationships I hold most dear. Honestly, I was embarrassed. We were there reliving a most amazing relationship I have shared with my father, and I couldn't describe the relationships I share with each of my kids. At that point, I said that I would have a proper response to the question the following day. As a father of five, I realized this would not be a quick download.

I have always tried to love and raise my children by giving each relationship similar weight and a consistent message. As individual personalities vary, so do relationships.

I spent the rest of that day, and most of the next morning, writing down thoughts and foundations I share with my children. I reached out to each of them to let them know what I was working on. I then asked them to write down a few thoughts from their own perspectives on our relationship. As I read their responses, my eyes were filled with tears of pride. It is here that my journey becomes very real and forever treasured.

From my daughter Casey

I am the luckiest girl in the world to have the most amazing relationship with my dad. He has guided me every step of the way.

My dad is the most supportive, loving, and encouraging and comforting dad . . . and he is the most amazing role model I could ask for. He tells me when I am wrong. He praises me when I am right. He is always patient with me. He always listens to me no matter the circumstance. He will always put his kids before himself.

Dad has taught me to work hard, be kind and respectful to others, and value family over everything.

I value his work ethic and his people skills.

He has given me the world. I am truly the luckiest girl.

I am certain Dad is the best dad there is, and I am grateful every day for that.

From my son Jack

My dad is my best friend. He is my role model. He is my moral compass.

We also share a gift that I truly believe no one else can relate to—having the name Jack Nicklaus. The name is truly an honor and a challenge. Everywhere I go in life, I am Jack Nicklaus's grandson first . . . and myself second. I have struggled with identity. Watching Dad handle this responsibility has been a playbook for me.

My grandfather has left an incredible legacy and, with that, a name that will forever echo in history. My father gifted it to me. And I can't wait to one day gift the name to my son and raise him the same way my father raised me.

From my son Will

The best way to describe you and me is with the term *doppelgängers*. On one hand, we are borderline identical with facial features and lanky torsos. On the other hand, the way you interact with life and aspire to make the five of us happy has had a significant impact on my purpose as a friend, brother, son, and human being.

You have taught me perseverance. You have taught me lessons

of family. You have always been a shoulder for me to lean on. Whether it's on the water, in the forest, on the sideline, or on the phone, you've always been there to give promising words of wisdom and life advice. Your stamp of approval means everything to me. I want to be like you.

From my son Charlie

My dad and I share a very special bond. Not just the kind that loves to hunt, fish, and hang out together, but the kind that means I can run anything by him . . . ask any question . . . and that is the law of the land. When he tells me to turn right, I turn right because I know he wants what's best for me. There is no second-guessing in our relationship. Dad has created an everlasting imprint on how I live my everyday life.

Most consider their dad just their dad . . . but mine is my best friend. I just hope I can be half the dad that he has been to me.

From my daughter Christie and her husband, Todger

Dad is one of my best friends, and his advice and love will always be held as of the utmost importance to me. I idolize how he has succeeded in life professionally, athletically, and, most importantly, with raising our family. He is loved by so many, and I am incredibly blessed to call him my father. I love you, Dad. I am so proud of you for this book and all your accomplishments.

Jack is the kind of man I want to be like. It is not because he's athletic, smart, and funny. It's because of his character. He stands for integrity, thoughtfulness, hard work, and overall love of family and life. These values that he lives by show through in every one of his children. In this world it is rare to find a great man to look up to, and I am blessed to have Jack as a father and a guide in my life.

To my children

You are everything to me. I am so very proud of you. You are my legacy. I am blessed because of you. I love you.

Acknowledgments

As much fun as it was to recall the many memories that were at the heart of this book, it took a great collection of resources to make it all come together.

Let me start by thanking the amazing John Maxwell, a leader in so many ways, who heard me tell some of these stories and encouraged me to put them all together. John even suggested who I needed to have as a writer, then made the call introducing me to *New York Times* bestselling author Don Yaeger. My partnership with Don was exactly what I needed, and we bonded as if we had known each other for years.

The next team that made this possible is the W Publishing Group at HarperCollins, where Matt Baugher, Damon Reiss, Kyle Olund, and Paula Major, along with the editorial, design, production, marketing, public relations, and sales teams kept everything moving.

Don and his writing and research team—Jim Henry and Kevin Derby—dug deep to find articles and resources, including work done by Bob Harig and Larry Schwartz of ESPN; Tom D'Angelo of the *Palm Beach Post*; Craig Dolch, a freelance sports writer in West Palm; Gary Van Sickle and Barry McDermott of *Sports Illustrated*; Tim Rosaforte with the Golf Channel; Steve DiMeglio of *Golfweek* and *USA Today*; *Golf Digest*'s Bob Verdi and Brian Wacker; and Golf.com's Charlie Mechem. We also learned from content on the websites of the PGA Tour, First Tee, Caddie Hall of Fame, and the USGA. The team at the Nicklaus Children's Health Care Foundation was wonderfully helpful.

Several family resources also were invaluable. The first is a set of scrapbooks my parents have kept over the years. The second is our great family friend Scott Tolley, who is Dad's manager and executive vice president for the Nicklaus Family Office. But the most important family resource is my mom, who kept both Don and me on the straight and narrow throughout the process! She fact-checked and edited our progress with precision and love that only a mom is capable of giving.

Last, but certainly not least, I want to thank my wife, Alli, and Don's wife, Jeanette, for supporting all the time we spent away working on these words. This truly was a team effort.

Notes

Introduction: Learning from the Golden Bear

1. Larry Schwartz, "This Bear Was Golden on the Links," ESPN .com, https://www.espn.com/sportscentury/features/00016385 .html.
2. "USGA Bob Jones Award," USGA.com, https://www.usga.org /content/usga/home-page/about/usga-bob-jones-award.html.
3. Jack Nicklaus II, in John Boehner, "3/24 Congressional Gold Medal in Honor of Jack Nicklaus," March 24, 2015, YouTube video, 43:20, https://www.youtube.com/watch?v=KQ7X2dUSwco.

Chapter 2: Attend Your Children's Games and Activities

1. William Arthur Harper, *How You Played the Game: The Life of Grantland Rice* (Columbia, MO: University of Missouri Press, 1999), 158.

Chapter 3: Raise Each Child Differently

1. Barry McDermott, "The Heir to the Bear," *Sports Illustrated*, March 11, 1985, https://vault.si.com/vault/1985/03/11 /the-heir-to-the-bear.
2. McDermott, "The Heir to the Bear."

Chapter 5: Act Like a Champion

1. Steve DiMeglio, "The Concession: It Has Been 50 Years Since Jack Nicklaus' Pivotal Ryder Cup Decision," *Golfweek*, September 20, 2019, https://golfweek.usatoday.com/2019/09/20/jack-nicklaus-explains-ryder-cup-concession-1969-tony-jacklin/.
2. DiMeglio, "The Concession."
3. Bob Harig, "Jacklin Fondly Recalls the '69 Cup," ESPN, September 15, 2004, https://www.espn.com/golf/rydercup04/news/story?id=1882137.

Chapter 6: See the Best in Others

1. "Company Overview," Nicklaus Companies, https://www.nicklaus.com/the-company/.
2. "Howard Milstein," Nicklaus Companies, https://www.nicklaus.com/the-company/leadership/howard-milstein/.
3. Bob Verdi, "The Ultimate Jack Nicklaus Interview," *Golf Digest*, June 23, 2020, https://www.golfdigest.com/story/the-ultimate-jack-nicklaus-interview.
4. May McNeer and Lynd Ward, *John Wesley* (Nashville: Abingdon Press, 1951), 79.

Chapter 7: Protect Your Name

1. John Maxwell, quoted in Don Yaeger, "Episode 8: John C. Maxwell, Leadership Expert, Asks: Do You Know the Top Time-Waster in Leaders' Lives?," in *Corporate Competitor Podcast*, produced by Savannah Gallagher, 42:25, https://donyaeger.com/corporate-competitor-podcast/episode-8/.
2. Zig Ziglar, *Staying Up, Up, Up in a Down, Down World* (Nashville: Thomas Nelson, 2004), 61.
3. H. Jackson Brown Jr., *Life's Little Instruction Book: Simple Wisdom and a Little Humor for Living a Happy and Rewarding Life* (Nashville: Thomas Nelson, 2012), 59.
4. Brian Wacker, "Jack Nicklaus Weighs In on Marking Golf Balls and Player Integrity," *Golf Digest*, April 5, 2017, https://www.golfdigest.com/story/jack-nicklaus-weighs-in-on-marking-golf-balls-and-player-integrity.

5. Wacker, "Jack Nicklaus Weighs In."
6. "About First Tee," First Tee, accessed January 6, 2021, https://firsttee.org/about/.
7. Jack Nicklaus, quoted in Chace Breitmoser, "The Golden Bear Talks to Congress About the Positive Impact of the First Tee," First Tee, August 19, 2014, https://firsttee.org/2014/08/19/golden-bear-talks-congress-impact-tee/.

Chapter 8: Be a Parent to Your Children First—and a Best Friend Later

1. Jack Nicklaus, "Letter to My Younger Self," *The Players' Tribune*, March 13, 2019, https://www.theplayerstribune.com/articles/jack-nicklaus-pga-letter-to-my-younger-self.
2. "16: Woody Hayes: Ohio State's Legendary Coach Tells Jack to Concentrate on Golf," PGA Tour: Mr. Columbus, accessed January 6, 2021, https://jack-columbus.pgatour.com/16-woody-hayes.

Chapter 9: Stay Laser-Focused on What You Can Control

1. Charlie Mechem, "6 Life Lessons That Jack Nicklaus Taught Me That Everyone Can Learn From," GOLF, September 12, 2020, https://golf.com/news/features/life-lessons-jack-nicklaus-taught-charlie-mechem/.

Chapter 10: Give More Than You Take in Your Relationships

1. "18: Family's Everything: Jack Was Determined to Be as Good a Father as a Golfer," PGA Tour: Mr. Columbus, accessed January 6, 2021, https://jack-columbus.pgatour.com/18-familys-everything.

Chapter 11: Build Your Legacy Every Day

1. Jack Nicklaus II, in John Boehner, "3/24 Congressional Gold Medal in Honor of Jack Nicklaus," March 24, 2015, YouTube video, 40:20, https://www.youtube.com/watch?v=KQ7X2dUSwco.

Chapter 12: Be Prepared So You're Mentally Tough

1. Mal Florence, "Chipping Away at History: Tom Watson's Winning Shot in 1982 U.S. Open Is Not Likely to Be Repeated,"

Los Angeles Times, June 14, 1992, https://www.latimes.com/archives/la-xpm-1992-06-14-sp-852-story.html.

Chapter 15: Be Ready to Seize Unexpected Opportunities

1. "Jack Nicklaus: Inducted in 1999," Caddie Hall of Fame, accessed January 6, 2021, https://caddiehalloffame.org/all-hall-of-fame-inductees/121-jack-nicklaus.

Chapter 16: Focus More on Your Family Than on Work

1. "Jack Was Determined to Be as Good a Father as a Golfer," PGA Tour: Mr. Columbus, accessed January 6, 2021, https://jack-columbus.pgatour.com/18-familys-everything.
2. "Jack Was Determined to Be as Good a Father as a Golfer," PGA Tour.

Chapter 17: Be Charitable and Don't Draw Attention to Yourself

1. Judy Martel, "The Nicklaus Family's Legacy of Philanthropy," *Jupiter Magazine,* April 24, 2020, https://www.jupitermag.com/jupiter-life/people/the-nicklaus-familys-legacy-of-philanthropy/.

Chapter 18: See the Bigger Picture

1. Paul Hornung, *The Story of Muirfield Village Golf Club and the Memorial Tournament* (Wilmington: Golden Bear Publishing, 1985), 176.

About the Authors

Jack Nicklaus II currently serves as president of Nicklaus Design and vice chairman of Nicklaus Company, and is the first of five children born to Jack and Barbara Nicklaus. A three-sport letterman in high school, Jack II went on to the University of North Carolina, where he played on the golf team. He had a brief career in professional golf, playing several years as a member of tours in Australia, Asia, and Canada, and on the European Tour. He also played in several PGA Tour events as a non-member. His career was cut short by rickettsioses, a tick-born sickness, but that directed him toward course design, where he has been recognized by selection into the prestigious American Society of Golf Course Architects. He works as both a solo designer and as a collaborator with his father and has designed nearly fifty golf courses that are open for play today. He serves on the board of directors of Nicklaus Children's Healthcare Foundation and is chairman of Muirfield Village Golf Club and chairman of the Memorial Tournament. Jack is married to Allison (Alli) and is the father of five—Jack, Christie, Charlie, Casey, and Will.

Don Yaeger is an eleven-time *New York Times* bestselling author, longtime associate editor at *Sports Illustrated,* and one of the most in-demand public speakers on the corporate circuit today. He delivers an average of seventy speeches a year to an average annual audience of nearly 100,000. He also hosts the popular *Corporate Competitor Podcast*. He lives in Tallahassee, Florida, with his wife and two children, ages eleven and twelve.

Nicklaus Children's Health Care Foundation

"The legacy you leave here on earth is measured by the hearts you touch."
—**Barbara Nicklaus,** Chairman and Co-founder

As young parents, Jack and Barbara pledged to each other that if they were ever in a position to help others, they wanted to help children. That promise ultimately led them to create the Nicklaus Children's Health Care Foundation. Established in 2004, the Foundation is a not-for-profit charitable organization focused on the advancement of pediatric health care. What started out as a labor of love has gained momentum and grown into a thriving charity, making a real difference for children locally and globally.

In 2015, in honor of the generous support of the Nicklaus Children's Health Care Foundation, Miami Children's Hospital was renamed Nicklaus Children's Hospital. Today, Nicklaus Children's Hospital serves as the Foundation's primary beneficiary. Helping children and families receive world-class health care is the invaluable gift of life that inspired the Nicklaus family more than fifty years ago.

Nicklaus Children's
Health Care Foundation

For more information or to make a donation, please visit **nchcf.org**.